Ticket Office

0 7 AUG 2025

South Western Railway
Axminster

On loan from . . . . .
please return. after reading . . .
Thanks
Alex,

YEOVIL TO DORCHESTER

Vic Mitchell and Keith Smith

MP Middleton Press

Cover picture: 4500 class 2-6-2T no. 5542 stands near Yeovil Loco Shed on 10th July 1956. The line to Dorchester is on the left and that to Yeovil Town is on the right. (R.C.Riley)

First published May 1990

ISBN 0 906520 76 2

Design - Deborah Goodridge
Laser typesetting - Barbara Mitchell

Published by Middleton Press
   Easebourne Lane
   Midhurst, West Sussex
   GU29 9AZ
   Tel. (0730) 813169

Printed & bound by Biddles Ltd,
   Guildford and Kings Lynn

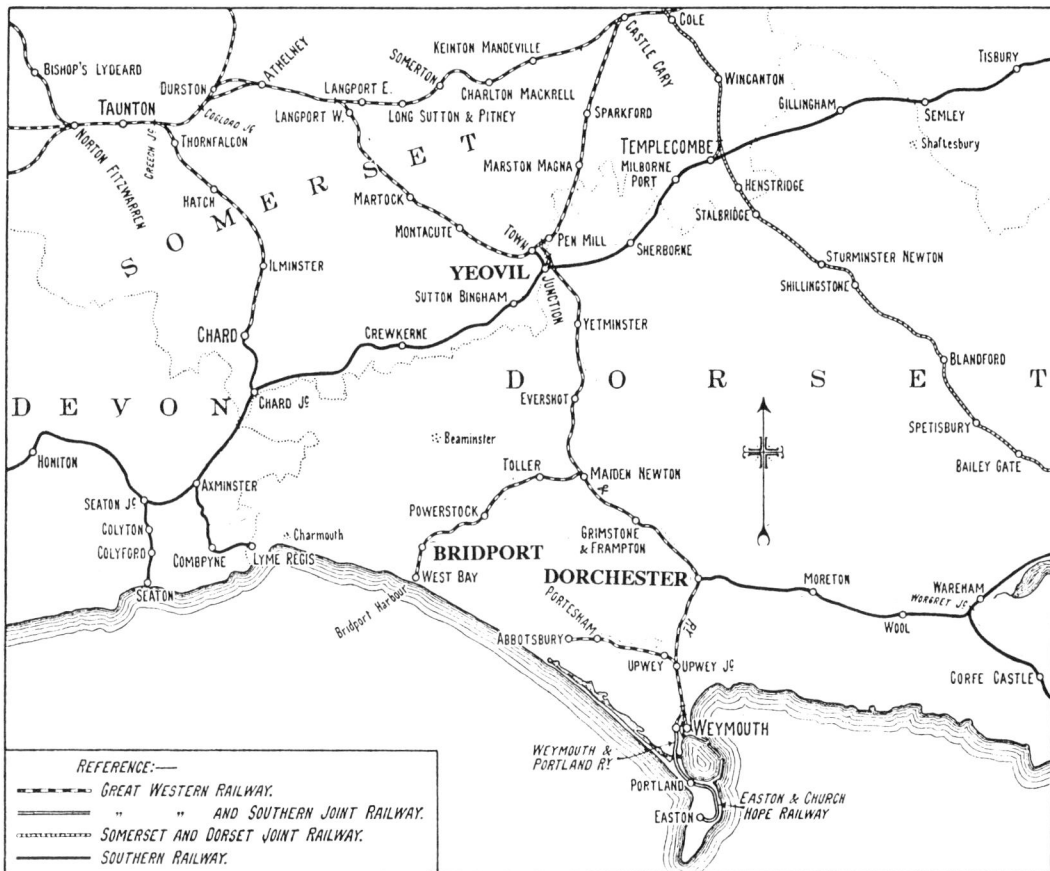

Map of the route and adjacent railways in 1932.
(Railway Magazine)

CONTENTS

ACKNOWLEDGEMENTS

We are extremely thankful for the help received from so many of the photographers mentioned in the captions and also for the assistance given by C.Attwell, G.Croughton, D.Cullum, M.K.Fellows, B.L.Jackson, N.Langridge, E.Staff, N.Stanyon and our ever supportive wives.

GEOGRAPHICAL SETTING

The route was built in areas drained by two important river systems. The northern catchment area is that of the River Yeo, which drains into the River Parrett at Langport which then flows into the Bristol Channel north of Bridgwater. South of the watershed, near Evershot, the land is drained by the River Frome, which enters Poole Harbour at Wareham.

The northern part is much faulted and presented complex geological problems for the railway engineers. For over a mile south of Yeovil Pen Mill, the line passes through a deep gorge cut through the thick Yeovil Sands by the River Yeo. The route then climbs steeply over a variety of faulted deposits to reach the chalk uplands of which much of Dorset is composed, and on which the remainder of the route is based.

The Bridport branch leaves the chalkland

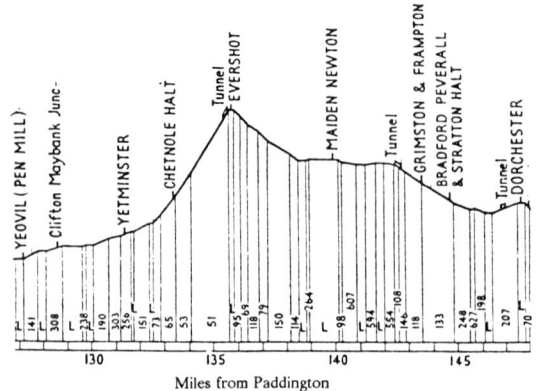

Miles from Paddington

at Toller and crosses a thick deposit of Fuller's Earth Clay for three miles, which caused stability problems in a cutting near the summit. Passing over a faulted area, the line descended onto the sands of the Bridport area.

HISTORICAL BACKGROUND

Authorisation to construct the route was included in the Wilts, Somerset & Weymouth Railway Company's Act of 30th June 1845. The company was sold to the Great Western Railway on 14th March 1850 and the line between Frome and Yeovil was opened on 1st September 1856. This broad gauge line was extended to Weymouth on 20th January 1857.

The London & South Western Railway reached Yeovil on 1st June 1860, the station becoming "Junction" when their branch to Yeovil Town opened on 1st June 1861.

Expansion

Initially only a single track was provided but this was doubled between Yeovil and Evershot in 1858. Between 18th and 22nd June 1874 the entire route, including the Bridport branch, was converted from broad to standard gauge. This brought extra traffic which had been previously routed from Weymouth to the Midlands and North via the LSWR, to avoid transhipment at the change of gauge. Doubling of the main line between Evershot and Maiden Newton took place in 1882. This was extended south to Grimstone & Frampton in 1884 and on to Dorchester in 1885.

Contraction

Two years after nationalisation in 1948, the route was transferred from the Western to

Southern Region of British Railways. In 1962, the policy was reversed, except that Dorchester West remained in the SR. Several intermediate stations were closed in 1966 and all freight services were transferred to the former LSWR route from Dorchester. Yeovil Town lost its passenger trains on 2nd October 1966. Reversion to single track between Yeovil Pen Mill and Maiden Newton took place on 26th May 1968, and south to Dorchester West on 9th June 1968. The service between Yeovil Pen Mill and Junction was introduced on 2nd October 1966 (upon closure of the Town station) and withdrawn on 5th May 1968.

Bridport branch

Trains began running between Maiden Newton and Bridport on 12th November 1857 and were extended to West Bay on 31st March 1884. As a wartime economy measure, passenger services on this extension were suspended between 31st December 1915 and 7th July 1919. They were withdrawn completely on 22nd September 1930 but goods services were retained until 3rd December 1962.

The branch lost its freight services on 5th April 1965 and its passenger trains on 5th May 1975.

PASSENGER SERVICES

The line opened with six trains a day and by 1869 there were five, with two on Sundays. By 1906, the frequency had doubled, this being temporarily halved in the latter part of WWI. Traffic developed during the 1920s and by the summer of 1934, the departures for Weymouth from Yeovil Pen Mill were as follows -

WEEKDAYS

am	Origin	Description
7.50	-	All stations to Dorchester
8.20	Bristol	Semi-fast
8.49	-	All stations
10.36	Bristol	Semi-fast
11.01	Bristol	Boat express
11.10	-	All stations - Sats. only
11.35	-	Maiden Newton - Not Sats.
pm		
12.01	Bristol	Express
1.10	Paddington	Semi-fast
1.35	Birmingham	Express - Sats. only
1.53	Bristol	All stations
3.23	Paddington	Semi-fast
4.19	Wolverhampton	Semi-fast
4.30	-	All stations
5.12	Westbury	Semi-fast
6.05	Paddington & Bristol	Monday, Fridays and Saturdays
7.12	Bristol	All stations
9.10	Paddington	Most stations
9.40	-	All stns. Thurs. & Sat.
10.29	-	Most stations

SUNDAYS

pm		
12.01	Bristol	Semi-fast
1.10	-	Express
1.19	Westbury	All stations
1.47	Wolverhampton	Semi-fast
5.47	Bristol	All stations
7.25	-	All stations

A similar service was operated until the end of the 1950s, except during WWII and the years of austerity that followed, but there was a greater number of holiday trains on Saturdays and more boat trains to Weymouth towards the end of the period.

The route was served by slip coaches from Paddington until September 1958. These were shed from West of England expresses at Westbury and often attached there to a Bristol-Weymouth service. Boat trains from the Midlands and London ceased to run after September 1959 and through running from Paddington ended in 1960.

The timetable for March 1961 showed twenty weekday and seven Sunday trains but by 1974 this was reduced to seven and six respectively, but on winter Sundays there was only one journey. In the summer of 1989, there were nine services Mondays to Fridays, with twelve on Saturdays and seven on Sundays.

Bridport branch

Until the line was extended beyond Bridport, there were four or five trains each way, weekdays only. In 1884, there were seven, three of which ran to West Bay. By 1906, the weekday service had increased to eight north of Bridport and ten to the south. There were three journeys between Maiden Newton and Bridport on Sundays, West Bay receiving only one. These were operated by the railmotor that was used on the Abbotsbury branch on weekdays.

Branch services were greatly reduced during much of WWI but, by 1925, they were back to eight weekday trips, four of which continued to West Bay. On Sundays, there was one return journey between Weymouth and Bridport only. By the summer of 1934, the branch had nine weekday and five Sunday trains.

Owing to the large military presence in the area, passenger services were maintained well during WWII, with ten weekday trains but only two on Sundays. By 1959, frequency had increased to twelve and eight respectively and in the year before closure, nine trips were operated, although on weekdays only, Sunday trains having been withdrawn in 1962.

September 1925

The 1904 survey at 6" to 1 mile has had the railway destinations added. At this time the double tracks of the GWR and LSWR were not connected to one another where they are shown to run parallel in the Yeo Valley. Earthworks and a bridge over the GWR are shown (lower right) which carried a LSWR spur between 1st January 1861 and 1st January 1870. The Clifton Maybank Branch (lower centre) is marked GWR and was in use between 13th June 1864 and 7th June 1937. It was used for the transfer of general goods between the companies, cattle being transferred at Yeovil Town. The earthworks to the south of the branch never received track, but may do so if plans come to fruition which would enable Weymouth line trains to use the spare platforms at Yeovil Junction.

YEOVIL PEN MILL

1. As at Frome, Dorchester and Weymouth, an overall roof was provided from an early date. The single track under it was used by the Durston line trains. (Lens of Sutton)

2. Another view of the overall roof includes a "Bulldog" at the head of a down train of clerestory coaches and some highly pointed lamps. (Lens of Sutton)

3. Looking towards Castle Cary we see the extent of the goods shed and a diamond crossing in the track leading to it. In the distance is North Box which closed on 14th February 1937. (Lens of Sutton)

The 1st edition is orientated so that the line to Castle Cary is on the right; that to Yeovil Town is upper left and the Weymouth route is lower left.

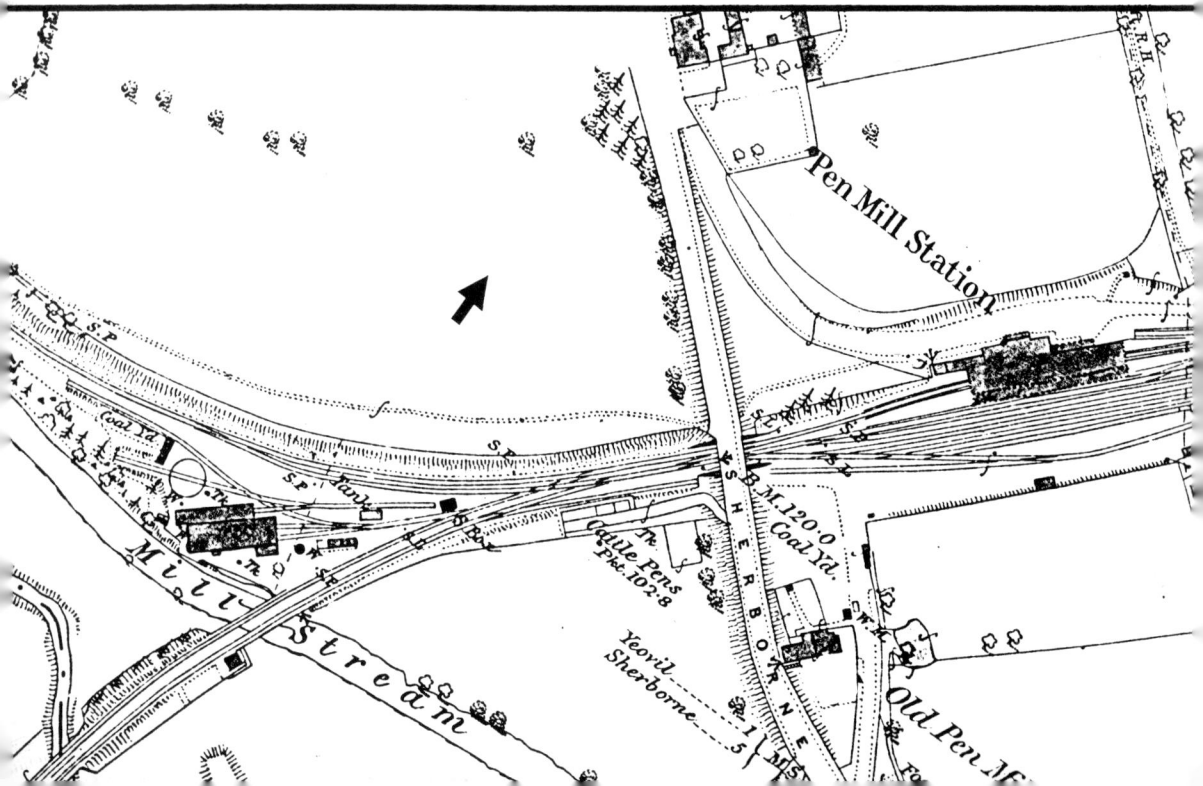

4. Representative locomotives of the SR and GWR are seen together on 13th June 1946. Class M7 0-4-4T no.129 waits with a train for Yeovil Town, while "Saint" class no.2955 *Tortworth Court* starts away with an express from Birmingham Snow Hill to Weymouth. (J.R.W.Kirkby)

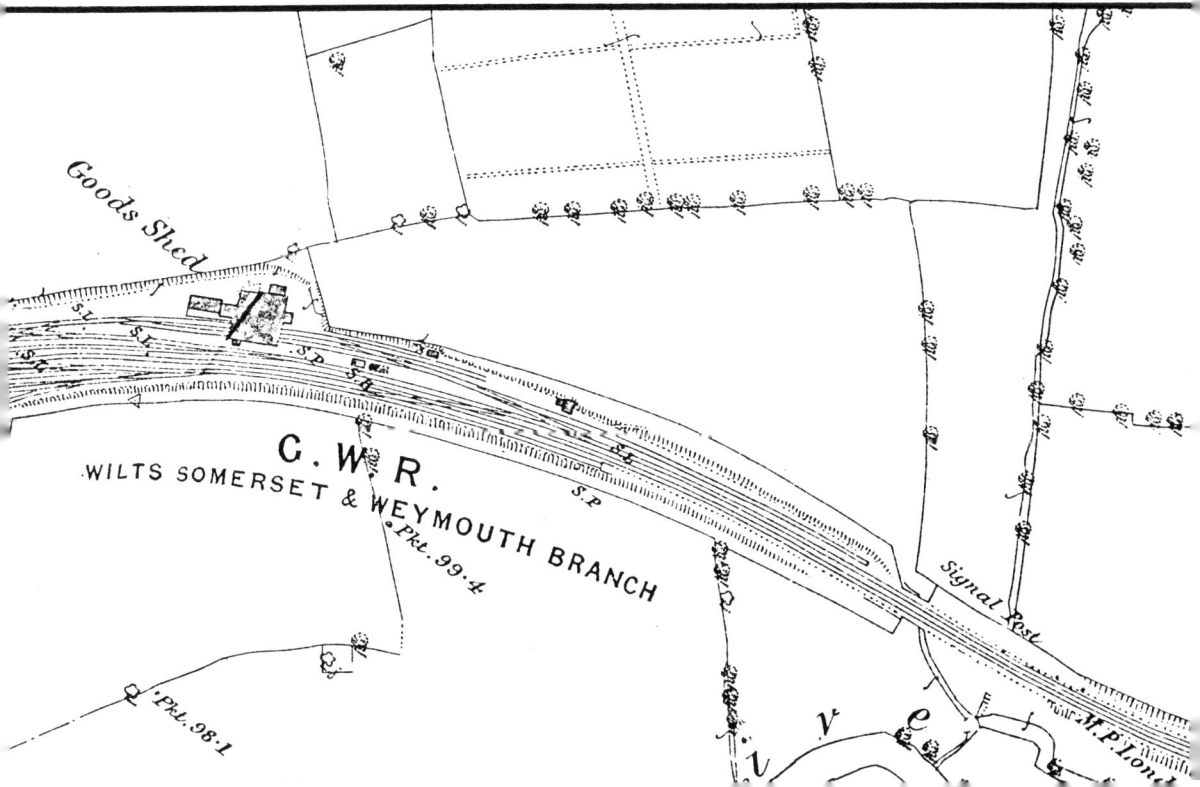

5. No. 6960 *Raveningham Hall* passes the 1937 signal box on 23rd August 1958. This locomotive was built in 1944 and now operates on the Severn Valley Railway. The Taunton branch train waits to the right. (A.E.Bennett)

6. Another August 1958 photograph shows the footbridge which was once inside the overall roof. The gas lamps, bookstall and pannier tank have long since disappeared. (A.E.Bennett)

YEOVIL PEN MILL

CHANGE FOR

TAUNTON & EXETER

```
Gt. Western Ry.    Gt Western Ry
        H.M. FORCES ON LEAVE
  Maiden Newton    Maiden Newton
              TO
            YEOVIL
          THIRD CLASS
  YEOVIL               YEOVIL
  FOR CONDITIONS SEE BACK  A
```
2727   2727

7. The route indicator must have been a welcome sight to weary enginemen on this wet day in August 1958. The locomotive has almost reached the shed. (A.E.Bennett)

8. On 3rd August 1959, young enthusiasts yearn for a footplate invitation but an inspector is watching. The goods yard once handled imported hides for the local glove making industry. (Lens of Sutton)

9. No. 6812 *Chesford Grange* waits to leave for Weymouth on 11th July 1964 with a train from Wolverhampton Low Level. Holiday traffic produced many extra and longer trains in July and August. (E.Wilmshurst)

10. The 10.20 Weymouth to Crewe "Perishables" on 9th July 1967 probably contained Channel Island tomatoes. No.34095 had lost its nameplate *Brentor* by then, as scrapping was imminent, steam operation ceasing the next day. (S.C.Nash)

11. Two gleaming coaches stand in the dock siding but the platform was not numbered or signalled for the use by passenger trains. The line at platforms 2 and 3 was signalled for reversible running. (Lens of Sutton)

12. A railcar leaves for Yeovil Junction on 4th May 1968, the last day of operation of the shuttle service, hence the presence of photographers in multiple. This service had only operated since 2nd October 1966, when Yeovil Town was closed. (E.Wilmshurst)

G. W. R.

Powerstock

TO

GRIMSTONE

G.W.R.

YEOVIL
(PEN MILL)

13. Since 1988, the signal box has controlled the entire route south to Maiden Newton, operated on the "No Signalman" key token system, Yeovil Pen Mill still retaining semaphore signalling. (C.L.Caddy)

14. Another 1972 architectural photograph illustrates the squat design, executed in the pleasing yellow stone used elsewhere in the locality. A footpath is now available to the Town Station car park, both having been constructed on former railway property. (C.L.Caddy)

16. Two-car Sprinter units operated most services on the route from 15th May 1989. Up and down trains are passing at Pen Mill on 2nd August 1989 while cycles are being loaded. Limited accommodation sadly means high charges and restrictions on this efficient form of transport. (J.H.Bird)

15. A connection has been retained between Yeovil Junction and Pen Mill, primarily for the use by trains diverted from the Paddington-Exeter main line. Two such trains are seen on 30th March 1985, when resignalling was in progress in the Taunton area. Beyond no.50037, a DMU waits between trips to Weymouth. (P.G.Barnes)

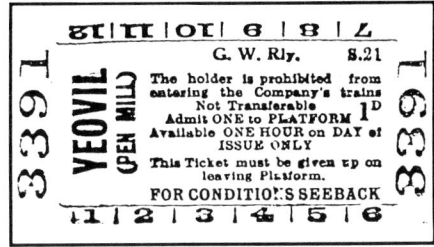

17. The entrance canopy has gone but a useful bus service was introduced in May 1988, linking Yeovil's two stations. This makes rail journeys between adjacent points of the compass a reality once again. (J.H.Bird)

Timetable showing the weekdays only service from May to October of 1989.

Yeovil Junction — Yeovil Pen Mill.
Bus service.

		SO	SO	SX	SO	SX	SO	SX	SO	SX	SO	SO	SX	SO	SX	SX	SO	SX
Yeovil Junction Station	145 d		09 27		09 30		11 35	11 40	12 16	13 37	13 35		15 37	15 35			17 35	19 30
Yeovil Bus Station	a		09 32		09 36		11 41	11 46	12 22	13 43	13 41		15 43	15 41			17 41	19 36
	d	07 45	08 28	09 33	09 37	10 05		12 10	12 23	13 44	14 00	14 40	16 00	16 10	17 05	18 00	18 00	
Yeovil Pen Mill Station	124 a	07 50	08 33	09 38	09 42	10 15		12 15	12 28	13 52	14 05	14 45	16 06	16 15	17 11	18 05	18 05	

		SO	SO	SX	SX	SX	SO	SO	SX	SO	SO	SX	SO	SX	SO	SX	SX	SO
Yeovil Pen Mill Station	124 d	08 00	08 41	08 45	09 50	10 45	10 05		12 36	12 40	14 28	14 28	15 00	16 38	16 38	17 40	18 20	18 25
Yeovil Bus Station	a	08 05	08 46	08 50	10 00	10 55	10 10		12 41	12 45	14 33	14 34	15 05	16 44	16 43	17 45	18 26	18 30
	d		08 47	08 51		10 56	11 05	11 56	13 00	13 10		15 00	15 06		17 00		18 27	
Yeovil Junction Station	145 a		08 53	08 56		11 02	11 11	12 02	13 05	13 16		15 06	15 12		17 06		18 40	

18. An indifferent quality photograph taken from Sherborne Road bridge is included to show South Box between the Yeovil Town line (right) and the Weymouth route (left). The box closed on 21st February 1937.
(Lens of Sutton)

19. The motive power depot, unclear in the previous picture, is viewed from the south in January 1959, the month in which it was closed.
(J.J.Smith)

20. Summer House Hill is again in the background of a shot from Sherborne Road bridge. On 30th March 1985, a diverted Paddington-bound train leaves the line from Yeovil Junction. This line runs parallel to the Weymouth one for nearly one mile.
(P.G.Barnes)

21. Yeovil South Junction was nearly half a mile south of Pen Mill and was opened on 13th October 1943 when connections were laid between the double tracks of the SR and GWR. Class M7 no.30131 propels the 10.18 Yeovil Town to Yeovil Junction on 2nd August 1959. (S.C.Nash)

22. Seen from the same position on the same day, no.34110 *66 Squadron* heads an Exeter to Weymouth excursion, which would proceed to Pen Mill for reversal. (S.C.Nash)

```
Gt. Western Ry.    Gt. Western Ry.
Grimstone&F'ton  Grimstone&F'ton
            TO
268  CATTISTOCK-Halt  268
       THIRD CLASS
        8½d C Fare 8½d C
Cattistock              Cattistock
    FOR CONDITIONS SEE BACK  F
```

```
Gt. Western Ry.    Gt. Western Ry.
Maiden Newton    Maiden Newton
            TO
569  YETMINSTER  569
       THIRD CLASS
        1/11 Z  Fare  1/11 Z
Yetminster              Yetminster
   FOR CONDITIONS SEE BACK    E.B
```

23. Ex-LNER no.60024 *Kingfisher* hauls the A4 Preservation Society's special train from Weymouth on 26th March 1966, towards Pen Mill where it will reverse. It will return along the adjacent track to Yeovil Junction, where it will reverse again before proceeding to Waterloo. (S.C.Nash)

24. The 14.20 Weymouth to Westbury "Perishables" approaches Yeovil South Junction on 9th July 1967, behind no.34052 *Lord Dowding*. The train was fully fitted (with brakes) and could therefore run at passenger train speeds. (S.C.Nash)

25. Forty minutes later, class 5 no.73092 passed the junction with a duplicate service. The trackbed of the former LSWR line to Yeovil Town curves away on the left. (S.C.Nash)

26. Looking in the opposite direction over, twenty years later, the Yeovil Town route is evident on the right. An up train from Weymouth is held at the home signal while no.50034 takes a diverted up train past it on 30th March 1985. (P.G.Barnes)

2nd · SINGLE   SINGLE · 2nd

2892

Grimstone & Frampton to
Grimstone&Frampton   Grimstone&Frampton
Weymouth   Weymouth

WEYMOUTH

(S)   1/11 FARE 1/11   (S)ʰ

For conditions see over   For conditions see over

2892

THORNFORD

27. No.7908 *Henshall Hall* begins the six mile climb from the Yeo Valley on 7th July 1962, hauling a train from Birmingham Snow Hill. Then officially a halt, the platforms served the village of under 400 people which is one mile to the east. (C.L.Caddy)

28. The staggered timber platforms were replaced by a single concrete one brought from Cattistock where it had become redundant following closure of the halt in 1966. This is the northward view in 1962. (C.L.Caddy)

29. A Plassermatic tamping machine passes on the up line on 22nd July 1966. This track was retained during the singling work two years later. (C.G.Maggs)

30. Sprinter no.150269 glides into Thornford, forming the 12.56 Bristol Temple Meads to Weymouth service on 2nd August 1989. Between 1942 and 1964, a siding for Beer Hackett Army Depot had been provided on the up side, 500yds south of the halt. (J.H.Bird)

YETMINSTER

31. The stone built station opened with the line and served the adjacent village, which by 1936 had a population of 520. This view towards Yeovil shows the presence of a staff crossing, not to be seen in later pictures.
(Lens of Sutton)

An additional siding was laid in 1932 to the milk factory, conveying United Dairies' tankers. This map shows the layout in the 1920s, the down refuge siding being 330yds in length, having been substantially extended in 1901.

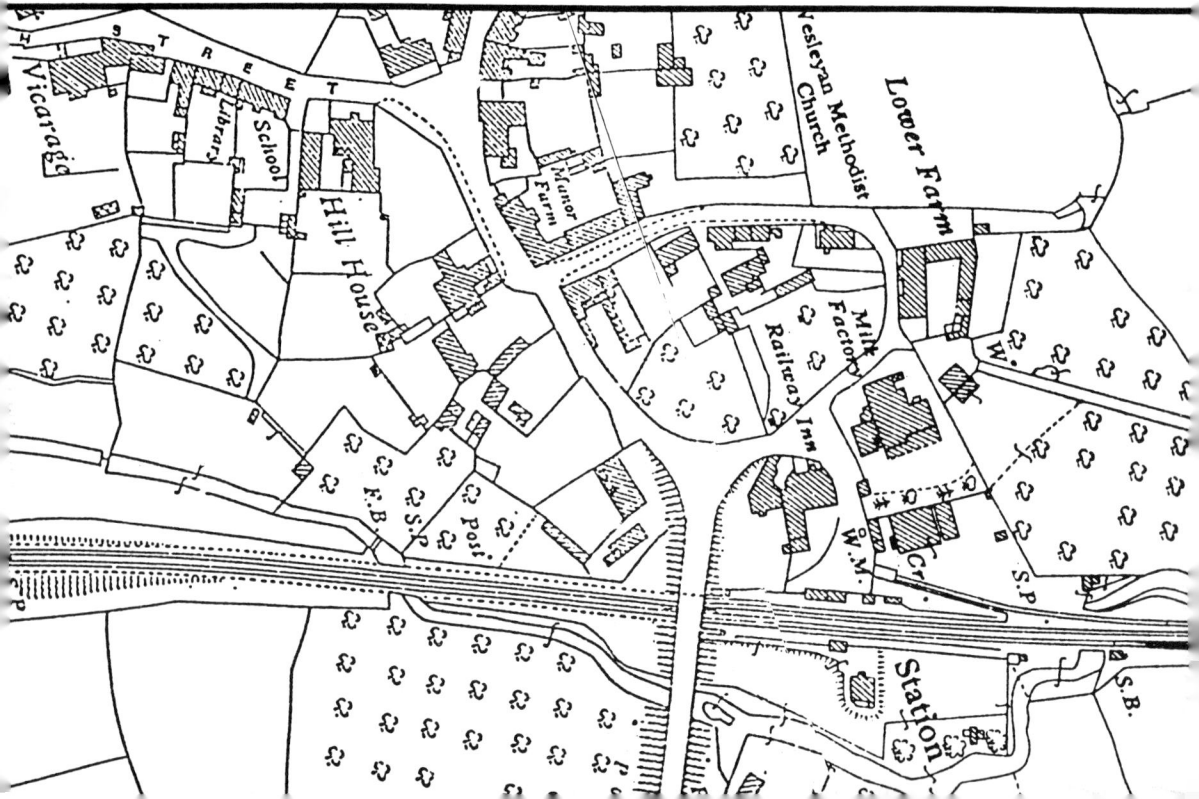

32. As at Thornford, steps were provided between the platforms and the road bridge and in 1990 trains stopped only by request. Here we look towards Dorchester. The station was unstaffed after 6th October 1969.
(Lens of Sutton)

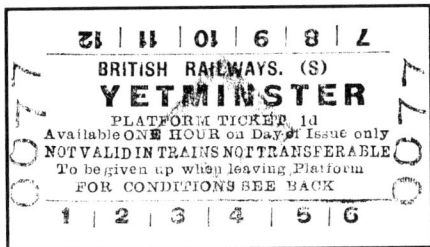

BRITISH RAILWAYS. (S)
YETMINSTER
PLATFORM TICKET 1d
Available ONE HOUR on Day of Issue only
NOT VALID IN TRAINS NOT TRANSFERABLE
To be given up when leaving Platform
FOR CONDITIONS SEE BACK
1 | 2 | 3 | 4 | 5 | 6

2nd - SINGLE   SINGLE - 2nd
Yetminster to
Yetminster   Yetminster
Chetnole Halt   Chetnole Halt
CHETNOLE HALT
(S)   6d. FARE 6d.   (S)
For conditions see over   For conditions see over

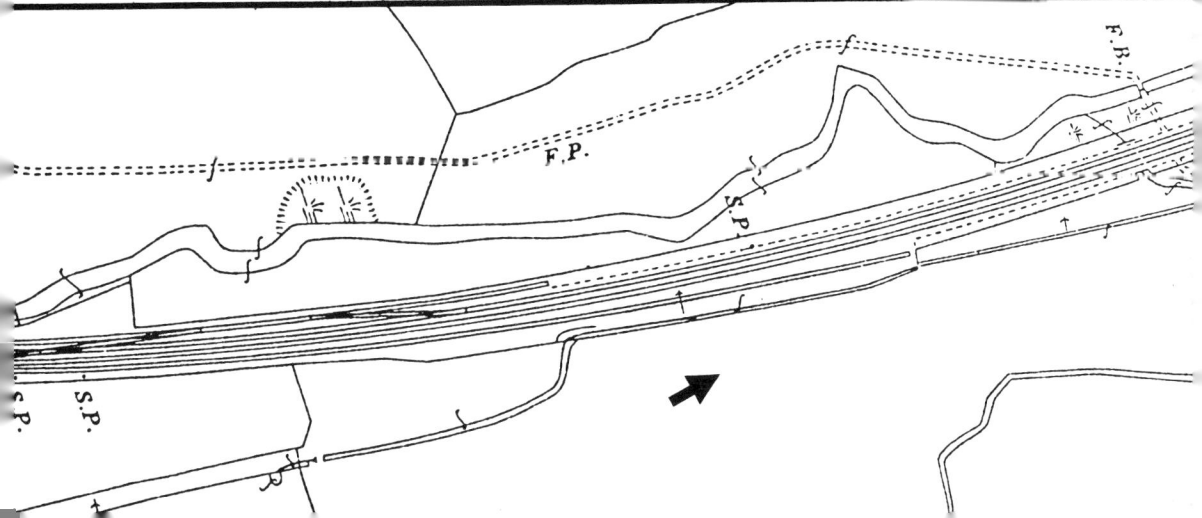

33. Viewed from the road bridge, much of the goods yard is visible. It contained a weighbridge, a 30cwt. crane and closed on 5th April 1965. (Lens of Sutton)

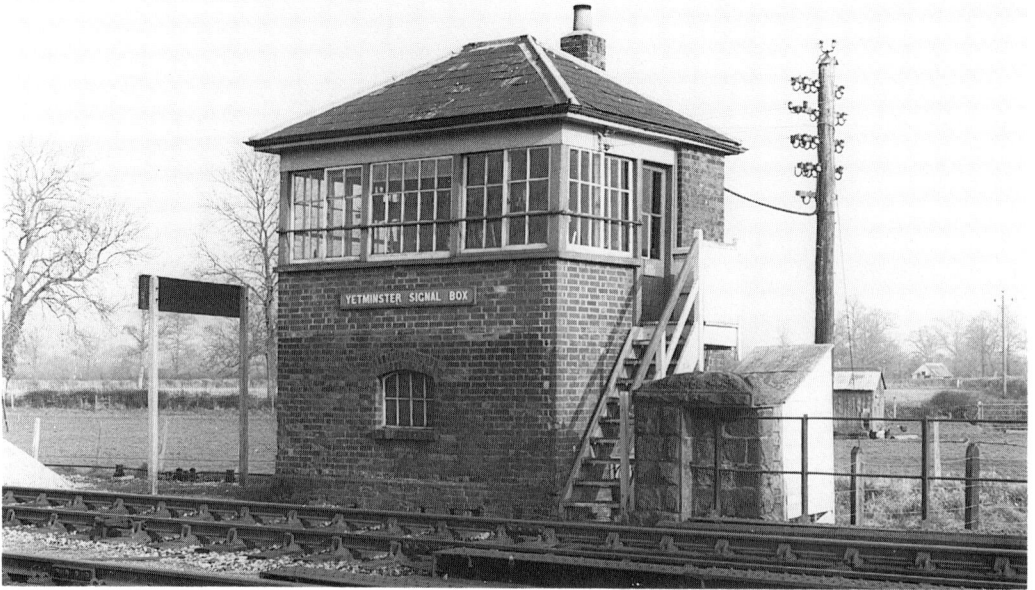

34. A tributary of the River Yeo (Wriggle River) passes under the line to the right of the signal box, which closed on 26th May 1968 when the down line was taken out of use. (C.L.Caddy)

35. No.5563 is seen under the loading gauge close to the river bridge on 7th July 1962. It was on banking duties, assisting down trains up to Evershot. (C.L.Caddy)

CHETNOLE

36. Opened on 11th September 1933, short timber platforms were erected on both sides of a road bridge, as at Thornford. Very few dwellings were within walking distance of the halt. (C.L.Caddy)

37. A further similarity to Thornford was that the original platforms were replaced with the other redundant one from Cattistock. No.155307 departs for Bristol on 2nd August 1989, by which time trains only stopped upon request. (J.H.Bird)

38. After climbing at 1 in 51 for nearly two miles, no.5099 *Compton Castle* approaches Evershot Tunnel, beyond which is the summit. At the rear, U class 2-6-0 no.31802 is banking this Cardiff to Weymouth excursion on 14th August 1960. (S.C.Nash)

39. Emerging from the south end of Evershot Tunnel (308yds long) on 24th June 1989 is the 13.30 Bristol Temple Meads to Weymouth service, formed of two 4TC sets propelled by no.33109. This stock made one return trip on Saturdays only during that summer. (P.G.Barnes)

EVERSHOT

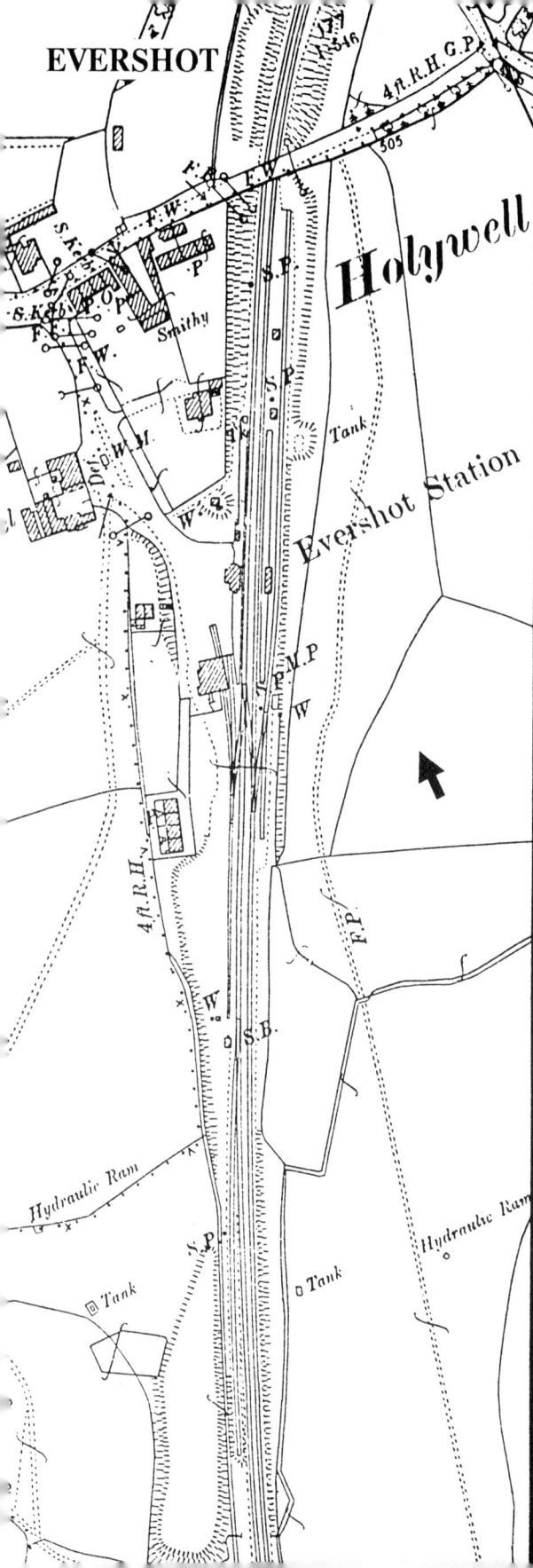

Holywell

Evershot Station

The 1902 edition marks the signal box (S.B.) in its earlier position, on the up side remote from the station. The crossover was moved further south and alterations made to the sidings in 1914.

40. Local landowners had been dictatorial with regard to the right to stop trains here. Maybe they also dictated that the station should be built of timber instead of stone and that the footbridge should carry ornate roofing. (Lens of Sutton)

41. A view towards Dorchester in 1965 includes the massive water tank and up platform column. Being at the summit of the line, about 500ft above sea level, locomotives were often low on water when they reached Evershot. (C.L.Caddy)

42. The signal box was closed on 7th January 1965 and was photographed a few weeks later when it had lost its nameboard. The station was built on the short level stretch of track at the summit. (C.L.Caddy)

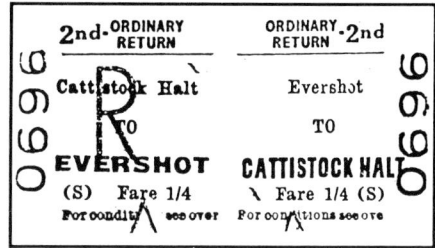

44. DMU no.50701 leads as the 11.15 Weymouth to Bristol Temple Meads passes through on 22nd July 1966. The cattle dock was obsolete but the railway cottages continued to perform a useful function. (C.G.Maggs)

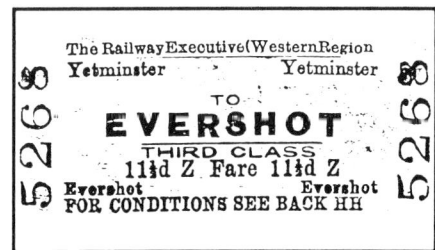

43. The station was closed on 3rd October 1966 and demolished during the following year. Water supply was by then also redundant, as steam haulage ceased that year. (C.L.Caddy)

CATTISTOCK

45. Over three miles from Evershot and nearly one mile to Maiden Newton, the halt was well situated to the small village. It was opened on 3rd August 1931 and rebuilt with pre-cast concrete components in 1959, when DMUs were introduced. This is a 1964 view, looking towards Yeovil. (C.L.Caddy)

46. No.D7095 roars through on 18th April 1964, with a Weymouth to Severn Tunnel Junction freight. The halt closed on 3rd October 1966 and the concrete components were re-used, as explained earlier. (C.L.Caddy)

47. The station opened with the line and the Bridport branch came into use later the same year. Its covered bay platform is on the right. (Lens of Sutton)

48. The signal box is seen in its earlier position on the down platform, which is surfaced with the grey chequered paving bricks for long beloved by the GWR. (Lens of Sutton)

3rd-SINGLE SINGLE-3rd

Maiden Newton To

Maiden Newton   Maiden Newton

Toller   Toller

TOLLER

(S)   6d   FARE   6d.   (S)

For conditions see over For conditions see over

0385

0385

49. After arrival from Bridport, the train would be reversed into the siding, as seen. The coach would remain there while the locomotive moved to the other side of the water tank, allowing the guard to run the coach back into the platform, under gravity. (Mowat coll.)

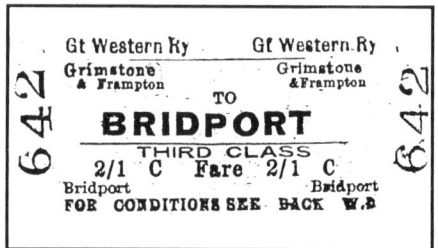

Gt Western Ry   Gt Western Ry

Grimstone   Grimstone
& Frampton   & Frampton
TO
BRIDPORT
THIRD CLASS
2/1 C   Fare   2/1 C
Bridport   Bridport
FOR CONDITIONS SEE BACK W.B

642   642

The 1st edition refers to an engine shed. This was a small shed which housed a stationary engine driving the water pump. The track layout changed remarkably little in the ensuing century.

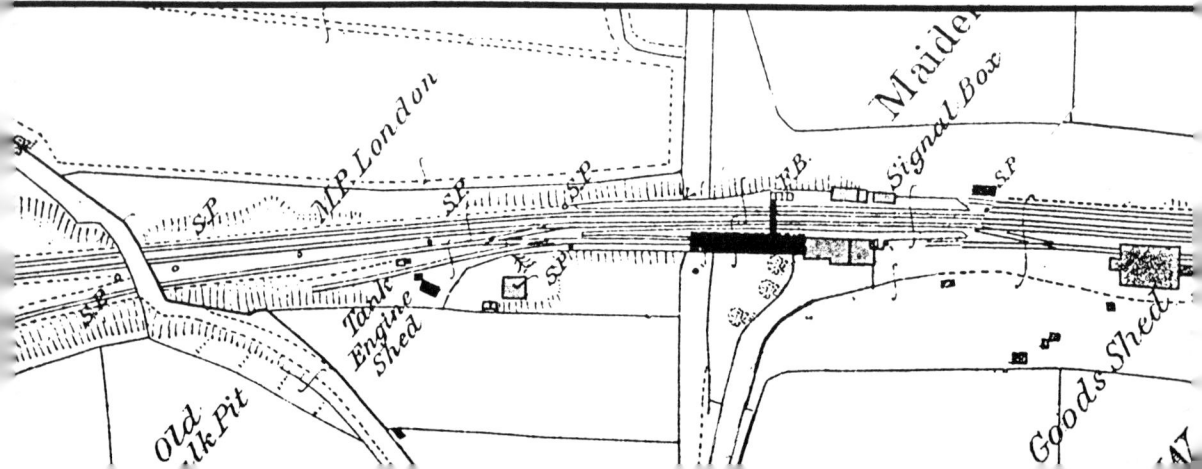

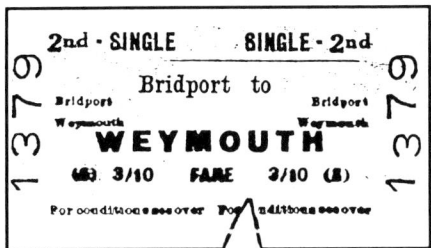

50. A mixed traffic 2-6-0, no.5364, is south-bound on 13th June 1946 and passes the connection with the Bridport branch, which runs under the left bridge span in the distance. (J.R.W.Kirkby)

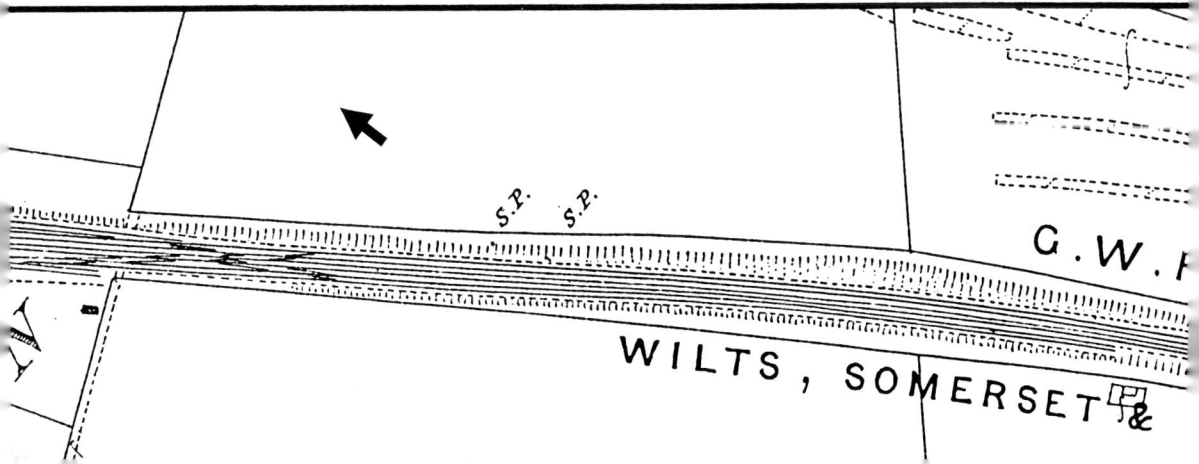

S.P.   S.P.

G.W.

WILTS, SOMERSET

51. A cattle truck stands at the dock by the pens as staff struggle over the crossing with milk churns. The goods shed was equipped with a 30 cwt crane but there was no crane in the yard, which closed on 5th April 1965. (Lens of Sutton)

MAIDEN NEWTON
FOR
BRIDPORT BRANCH

52. A Yeovil to Weymouth stopping train clatters over the crossover on 31st March 1956. The bridge carries the road which runs over the hill to Cerne Abbas. (J.W.T.House/C.L.Caddy)

53. Class 1400 0-4-2T no.1418 passes the cattle dock in August 1957, while working a Weymouth-Yeovil stopping service. On Sundays, the auto train would work the Bridport branch. (E.Wilmshurst)

MAIDEN NEWTON
FOR
BRIDPORT BRANCH

54. A rare visitor was class M7 no.30107, which appeared on a Railway Enthusiasts Club Special on 7th June 1958. It looks at home with the SR style lampshades, which appeared during the period of Southern Region responsibility. (J.W.T.House/C.L.Caddy)

55. The all stations and halts to Weymouth leaves at 4.20pm on 5th May 1959, hauled by no.7780. During the following summer this train started at Maiden Newton at 4.30pm and only ran on Saturdays. (S.C.Nash)

56. The Southern Counties Touring Society had poor weather on 25th August 1963 for its "Hants & Dorset Enterprise". The tour from Waterloo ran via Weymouth, Westbury and Salisbury, also various branches. Ex-LNER class A3 no.60112 *St. Simon* struggles with a 7-coach train on wet rails. The train had run to West Bay behind two 0-6-0 PTs, nos.4689 and 7782. (S.C.Nash)

57. Contrasting liveries were evident in November 1965 as a Bristol bound DMU displays its yellow panel while the single car for Bridport carries its original lined green colour scheme. (J.A.M.Vaughan)

58. As in the previous photograph, the main line signals are not next to the track to which they refer, owing to the curvature of the line causing visibility problems. The signals for the driver of this railcar arriving from Bridport on 18th March 1967 are above the 15 and 10 speed restriction signs. Beyond the tank traps are the buffers of the long down refuge siding. (C.L.Caddy)

59. In April 1968, the branch junction was altered to prevent through running. Compare this July 1970 view with the previous photograph and note that the SR style signal has been replaced by a GWR type, but facing the other direction. (C.L.Caddy)

61. One semaphore and one colour light signal are visible as a DMU departs for Weymouth on 13th July 1970. Twenty years on, the single siding was still retained by the engineers, access being controlled by a ground frame. Fuel for the local coal merchant arrived by road. (J.H.Bird)

60. The knapped flint structure seems at home in its chalk downland environment and is seen in 1968, although it remained little altered over 20 years later. (C.L.Caddy)

62. The loss of the roof was no doubt regretted on 4th April 1975, when late snow made life difficult. Note that the lattice footbridge had been replaced by a SR style concrete one. (C.L.Caddy)

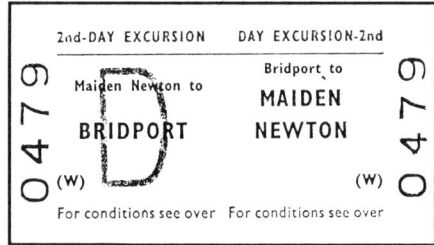

64. Class 50s were quite often used on the route prior to the introduction of class 37s. No.50031 speeds south on 22nd October 1983 with the "Wessexman", a railtour organised by the Class 50 Preservation Society. Only one ground signal then remained. (J.A.M.Vaughan)

63. The 12.17 to Bridport passes the former station master's house on 23rd April 1975, two weeks before closure of the branch. By then, local housing was spreading towards the railway but the tank traps remained. (J.Scrace)

65. The 17.35 Weymouth to Bristol Temple Meads service on 1st July 1989, passes the former 57-lever 1921 signal box, which had ceased to function as such twelve months earlier. Subsequently it was used by the Permanent Way Dept. (A.Dasi-Sutton)

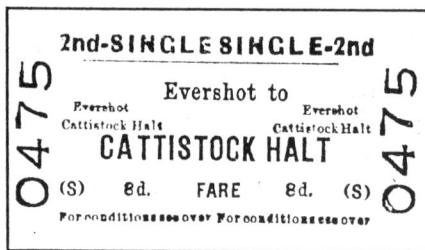

2nd-SINGLE SINGLE-2nd

Evershot to

Evershot
Cattistock Halt

Evershot
Cattistock Halt

CATTISTOCK HALT

(S)   8d.   FARE   8d.   (S)

For conditions see over For conditions see over

0475   0475

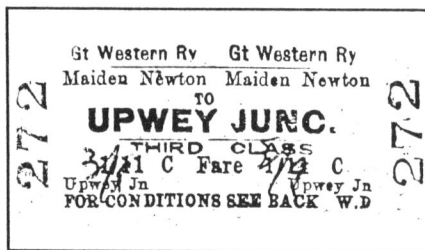

Gt Western Ry   Gt Western Ry

Maiden Newton   Maiden Newton
TO

UPWEY JUNC.

THIRD   CLASS

Upwey Jn   C   Fare   C   Upwey Jn
FOR CONDITIONS SEE BACK   W.D

272   272

67. The box on the left is the ultimate in miniaturisation of a self-service signal box. The driver of the class 155 Sprinter waits to obtain the token to proceed to Yeovil, while no.47572 *Ely Cathedral* arrives with the 9.10 from Bristol on 30th July 1989. The equivalent train on weekdays was class 37 hauled and, together with the class 33 Saturdays only working seen in the previous picture, comprised the only locomotive hauled trains on the route that summer. (V.Mitchell)

66. With no signals in sight, no.33116 departs sith 4TC no.8028, forming the 17.05 from Weymouth. The leading coach has hopper windows in the front half only. (C.Wilson)

The Bridport Branch

68. In its final years, the branch survived on a service provided by single railcars, such as this one seen on 13th July 1970 approaching the main line, having just passed under the Cattistock road. (J.H.Bird)

69. The station was opened on 31st March 1862 to serve the adjacent village of Toller Porcorum but not the even smaller Toller Fratrum, one mile to the east and with easier access to Maiden Newton station. The ground frame (in the hut on the left) was moved closer to the points on 26th June 1946.
(Lens of Sutton)

The 1902 maps indicates the presence of a single siding. This was extended west to form a loop in 1905. "Porcorum" suggests that the Romans bred pigs here.

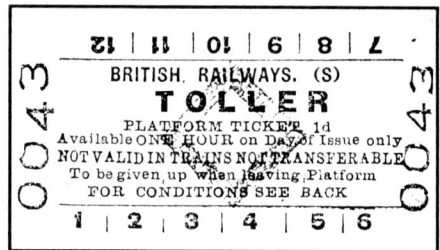

BRITISH. RAILWAYS. (S)
TOLLER
PLATFORM TICKET. 1d
Available ONE HOUR on Day of Issue only
NOT VALID IN TRAINS NOT TRANSFERABLE
To be given up when leaving Platform
FOR CONDITIONS SEE BACK

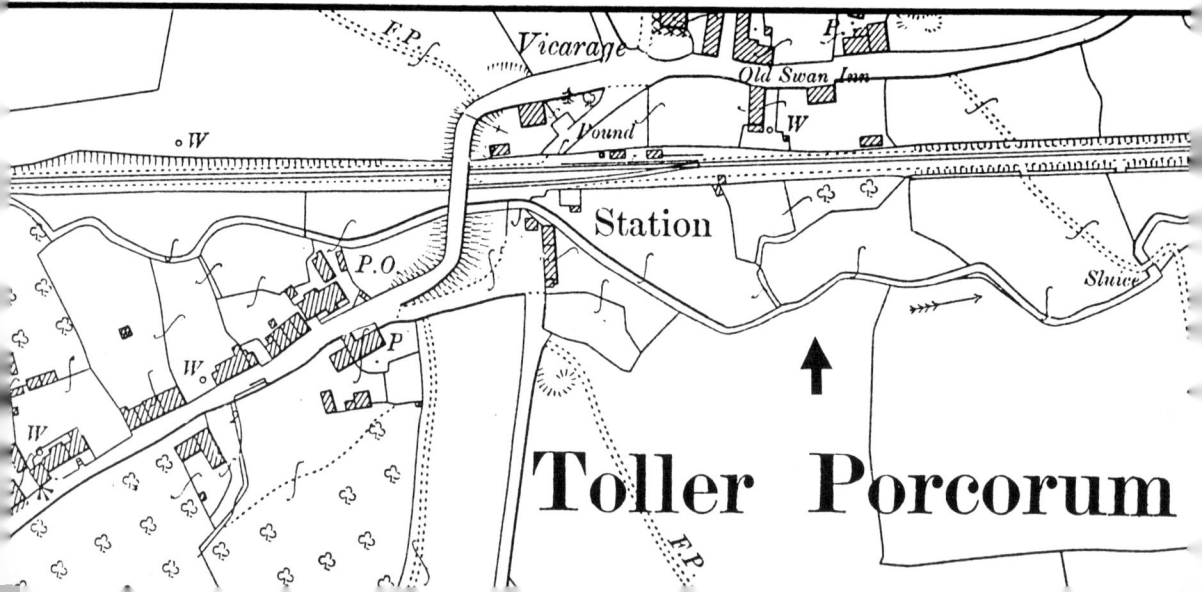

Toller Porcorum

70. The extent of the goods loop can be seen in this March 1956 photograph - freight facilities were withdrawn on 4th April 1960. The structure on the right is an open-top cast iron urinal. (J.W.T.House/C.L.Caddy)

```
┌─────────────────────────────────────────┐
│      Gt Western Ry    Gt Western Ry      │
│ ∞   Powerstock        Powerstock     ∞   │
│ LΩ            TO                      LΩ  │
│ 4         TOLLER                      4   │
│        THIRD   CLASS                      │
│        8½d  Z  Fare  8½d  Z               │
│  TOLLER                      TOLLER       │
│  FOR CONDITIONS SEE BACK H H              │
└─────────────────────────────────────────┘
```

← — — — —

71. The station was boarded up following withdrawal of staff on 11th April 1966. Local traffic had included watercress (to the Midlands and North), wooden boxes (to the growers of Kent) and timber for sleepers and pit props. (J.Scrace)

← — — — —

72. Two more 1975 views show the delightful scenery and the picturesque environs of the station, together with the position of the road relative to them, prior to the erection of the bridge over the railway. The building had been erected in 1905, when the platform was lengthened at the north end. (J.Scrace)

73. The last day of operation was 5th May 1975 and on that occasion a 3-car unit had to be added to the single car to carry the numerous sentimental travellers. Two extra journeys were made. (J.A.M.Vaughan)

POWERSTOCK

74. When the branch opened, this was the only intermediate station and was known as "Poorstock", until 1860. A former quarry provided a site for the three sidings of the goods yard, which closed on 13th March 1961. The building has been in residential use since 1970. (Mowat coll.)

```
  ┌────────────────────────────────────────────┐
  │     2nd · SINGLE      SINGLE · 2nd          │
  │  ∞        Bridport   to          ∞          │
  │  ∞   Bridport              Bridport   ∞     │
  │  5   Powerstock           Powerstock  5     │
  │  ∞   POWERSTOCK            ∞                 │
  │  5  (S)   8d.    FARE    8d.   (S)   5       │
  │     For conditions see over For conditions see over │
  └────────────────────────────────────────────┘
```

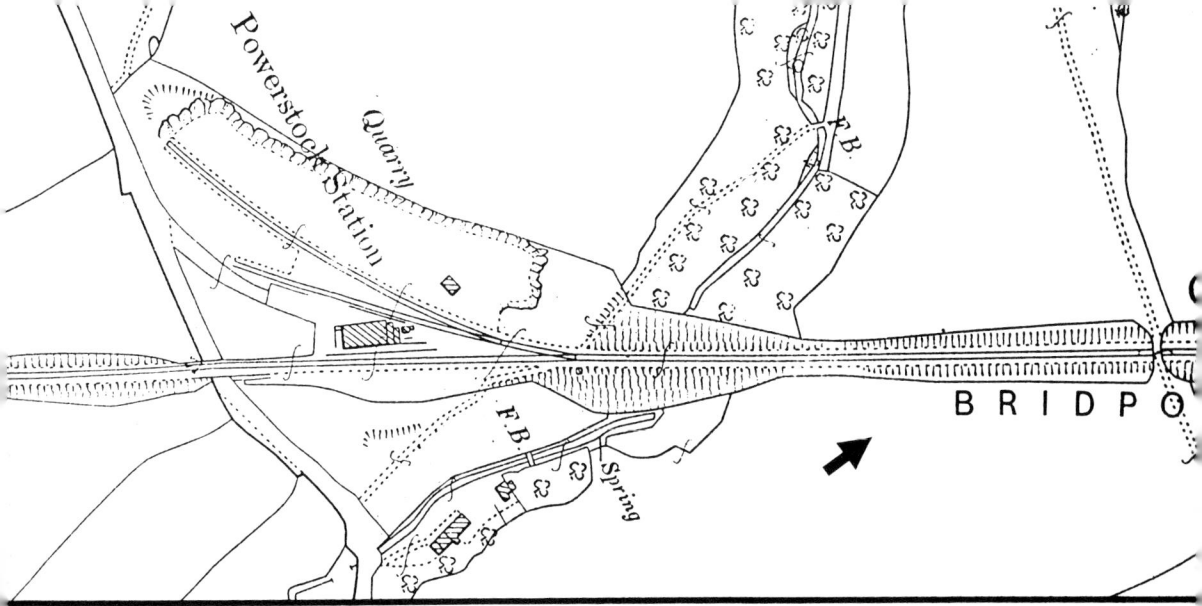

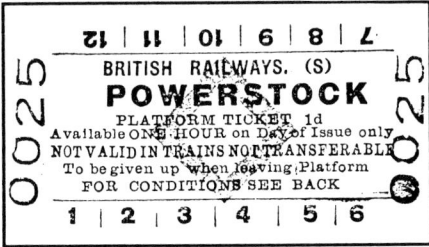

The 1902 survey shows only two of the ultimate three sidings.

BRITISH RAILWAYS. (S)
POWERSTOCK
PLATFORM TICKET 1d
Available ONE HOUR on Day of Issue only
NOT VALID IN TRAINS NOT TRANSFERABLE
To be given up when leaving Platform
FOR CONDITIONS SEE BACK

0025

75. Staffing ceased on 11th April 1966 and on 22nd January 1967, the LCGB operated the "Bridport Belle", seen headed by 2-6-2T no.41320 and banked by no.41295. The train stalled; no.41320 ran short of water and diesel no.D6541 was summoned to assist. This was the last steam to be seen on the branch. (J.Scrace)

76. On the outskirts of Bridport, at Bradpole, a road was crossed and in the final years, the guard was obliged to open and close the gates, as witnessed here on 1st October 1969. Temporary military sidings were provided here and near Loders during WWII, for use by rail mounted guns. (J.A.M.Vaughan)

March 1961

Table 70		MAIDEN NEWTON and BRIDPORT															
Miles		**WEEK DAYS**															
		am	am		am		pm		pm		pm		pm		pm	pm		pm	pm		pm
	Maiden Newton ... dep	8 15	1012	..	1127	..	1212	..	1 12	..	2 20	..	3 20	..	4 15	..	5 12	6 35	..	8 17	9 15	..	10 9
2	Toller	8 20	1017	..	1132	..	1217	..	1 17	..	2 25	..	3 25	..	4 20	....	5 17	6 40	..	8 22	9 20	....	1014
5¼	Powerstock	8 26	1023	..	1138	..	1223	..	1 23	..	2 31	..	3 31	..	4 26	..	5 23	6 46	..	8 28	9 26	..	1020
9¼	Bridport .... arr	8 33	1030	....	1145	..	1230	..	1 30	....	2 38	..	3 38	....	4 33	....	5 30	6 53	....	8 35	9 33	....	1026

Miles		**WEEK DAYS**															
		am		am	am		am	pm		pm		pm		pm		pm		pm	pm		pm	pm		pm
	Bridport ... dep	7 30	..	9 7	11 4	..	1149	1236	..	1 35	..	2 50	..	3 52	..	4 40	5 58	..	7 40	8 50	..	9 40	1032
3¼	Powerstock	7 36	..	9 13	1110	..	1155	1242	..	1 41	..	2 56	..	3 58	..	4 46	6 4	..	7 46	8 56	....	9 46	1038
6¾	Toller	7 43	..	9 20	1117	..	12 2	1249	..	1 48	..	3 3	..	4 5	..	4 53	6 11	..	7 53	9 3	....	9 53	1045
9¼	Maiden Newton ... arr	7 50	....	9 25	1122	..	12 7	1254	..	1 53	....	3 8	....	4 10	..	4 58	6 16	..	7 58	9 8	....	9 58	1050

		SUNDAYS								**SUNDAYS**			
		pm		pm		pm		pm				pm		pm		pm		pm
Maiden Newton ... dep	2 36	..	3 42	..	6 40	..	7 45	..	Bridport ... dep	3 15	..	4 10	..	7 12	..	8 22	..
Toller	2 41	...	3 47	..	6 45	..	7 50	....	Powerstock ...	3 21	..	4 16	...	7 18	..	8 28	..
Powerstock	2 47	..	3 53	..	6 51	..	7 56	..	Toller	3 28	..	4 23	..	7 25	..	8 35	..
Bridport .... arr	2 54	..	4 0	..	6 58	..	8 3	....	Maiden Newton ... arr	3 33	..	4 28	...	7 30	..	8 40	....

BRIDPORT

77. A new signal box was built in 1894 and sited on the platform. This fact helps to date the photograph, which includes an example of bridge rails, which were mounted on longitudinal timbers with iron tie rods and well spaced sleepers. (Lens of Sutton)

78. A view from the south end shows the loop behind the 1894 down platform and a substantial wooden signal post, typical of the period. The station was named Bridport Bradpole Road from 1887 until 1902. (Lens of Sutton)

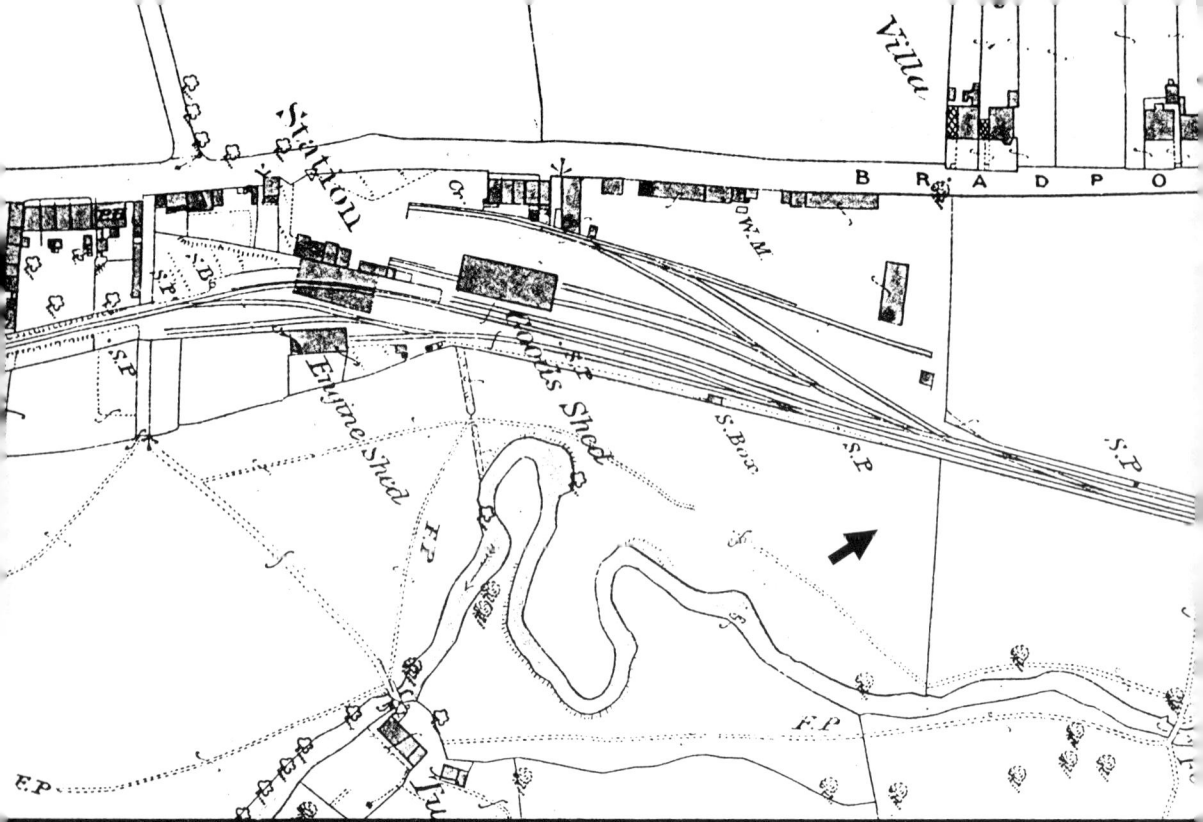

The 1st edition marks the original position of the signal box and shows the 1884 extension to West Bay, on the left, curving under the overall roof which lasted until 1894.

79. No less than thirteen "Small Prairies" still exist, but not no.4562. It is seen in 1956, standing in the goods yard which closed on 5th April 1965. (J.W.T.House/C.L.Caddy coll.)

80. The additional dock siding on the left was provided in 1909 and was known as Coronation Siding. The signal was erected during the Southern Region regime. No.8799 is shunting stock on 6th October 1956, the down platform canopy having been removed in 1952. (S.C.Nash).

The 3rd edition of about 1930 indicates the presence of cattle pens and a crane, which was of 6 ton capacity. Until 1884 there were two straight terminal platforms.

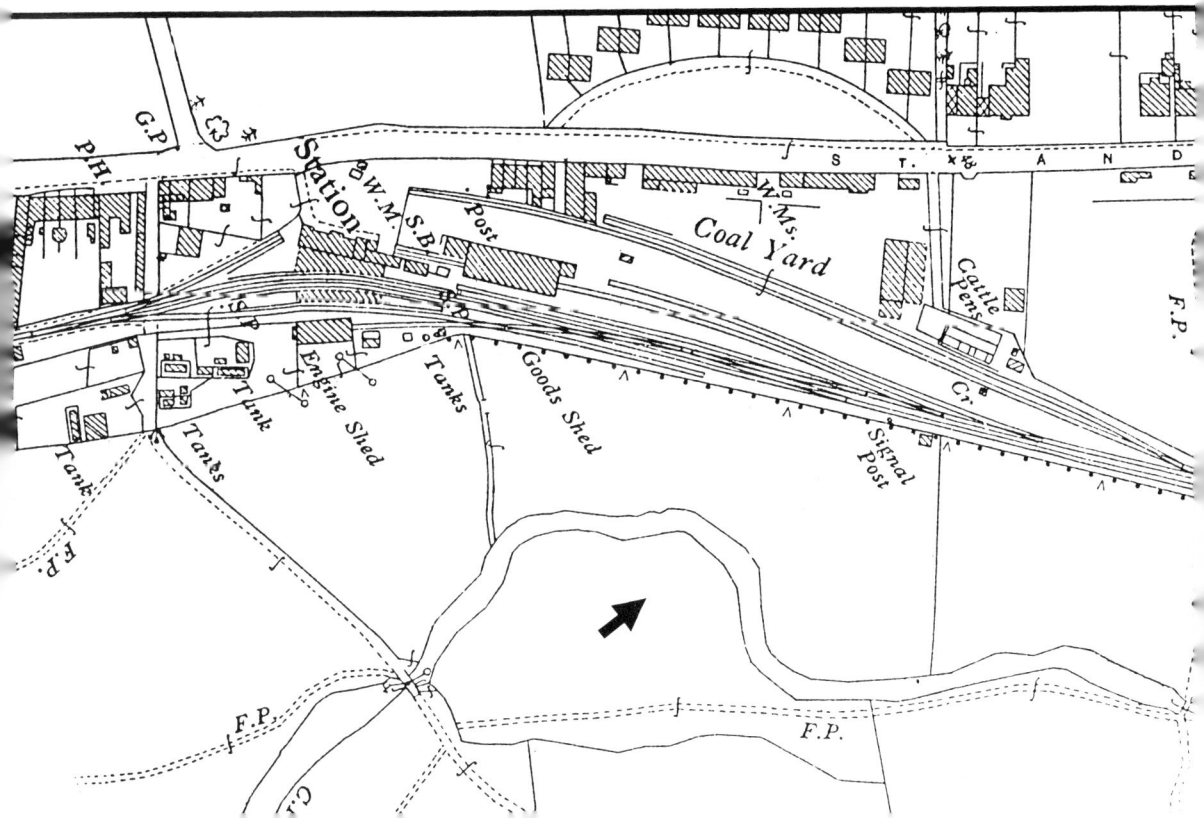

81. The signalman collects the staff from an arrival, while another train waits in the back road in August 1957. In the background is one of the few straight sections of track on the branch. All trains arrived at the down platform. (E. Wilmshurst)

MAIDEN NEWTON and BRIDPORT

Miles	Down	Week Days									Suns				Miles	Up	Week Days									Suns			
	HOUR ☞	8	9	11	12	1	3	4	7	9	11	12	2	5	6	9		HOUR ☞	6	8	10	11	12	3	4	7	9	9	2	4	5	8
										N		X	M	X	X	X											N	X	M	X	X	X
—	Maiden Newton ...dep.	10	40	10	25	47	50	55	45	38	44	11	2	20	41	—	Bridport ....dep.	30	50	30	40	50	0	15	10	5	40	50	35	35
2¼	Toller.................	17	45	15	30	52	55	55	0	50	43	.	18	.	.	46	Powerstock	40	58	38	48	58	8	23	18	13	48	59	.	.
5¼	Powerstock	26	52	22	37	59	2	2	7	57	50	.	26	.	.	53	Toller.................	55	6	46	56	6	16	31	26	21	56	8	.	.
9¼	Bridport C ....arr.	37	0	30	45	7	10	10	15	5	58	4	35	22	40	1	9	Maiden Newton 2, 8 arr.	5	11	51	1	11	21	36	31	26	1	13	55	55	20

C Sta for Lyme Regis **M** Rail Motor Car, one class only **N** Thurs and Sats **X** 3rd class only

Where the MINUTES under the Hours change to a LOWER figure and DARKER type it indicates the NEXT HOUR

August 1934

82. The REC railtour, seen earlier at Maiden Newton, pauses in the down platform on 7th June 1958 to allow participants to examine the station in detail. Note that the point rodding passes under the check-railed tracks, in the foreground. (R.M.Casserley)

83. The small depot was a sub-shed of Weymouth and closed on 15th June 1959. The pit and ash wagon are seen on 5th May 1959, along with 2-6-2T no.4507. A shedmaster's report of 1888 stated that the turntable had been "long filled in". (S.C.Nash)

84. A few minutes after the previous picture was taken, no.4507 was ready to receive coal from a tub. Behind is the water tank which was replenished from the nearby River Asker. (S.C.Nash)

85. No.3737 waits with a train of predominantly empty coal wagons on 27th April 1963. Coal had always been an important traffic inwards and goods outwards had earlier included locally produced rope and sail cloth. At this time, the goods engine worked the coaches on the left once a day to Maiden Newton, all other services having been diesel operated since 6th April 1959. (C.L.Caddy)

86. The box had a 27-lever frame and an electric train staff instrument to control single line working. Opened in 1894, it was closed on 8th June 1965. (C.L.Caddy)

87. In 1963 posters on the slate-roofed stone building included one for cheap tickets to Yeovil for football and one for local bus services. The campaign to eliminate rail passengers was starting. (C.L.Caddy)

0342   7 | 8 | 9 | 10 | 11 | 12
British Transport Commission (S)
BRIDPORT
PLATFORM TICKET 2d.
Available one hour on day of issue only.
Not valid in trains. Not transferable.
To be given up when leaving platform.
For conditions see over
1 | 2 | 3 | 4 | 5 | 6   0342

88. In 1959, three car DMUs were used, these being replaced by two car sets and by 1965 only single cars were required. Closure was scheduled for 3rd October 1966, but was deferred and a further reprieve was granted on 4th June 1967. This is the scene in July 1970. (J.H.Bird)

89. The station was unstaffed after 6th October 1969 and the premises became neglected, further discouraging passengers. Antique gas lighting remained to the end. (J.H.Bird)

90. Two final photographs show the sad state shortly before the closure on 5th May 1975. The signal box once stood beyond the milepost and a siding ended close to it. (C.L.Caddy)

91. The end in all senses, especially for the oil lamp on the buffers. There is now no trace of the station, the entire site being occupied by commercial premises. The station was last painted in 1957 - green and cream. (J.Scrace)

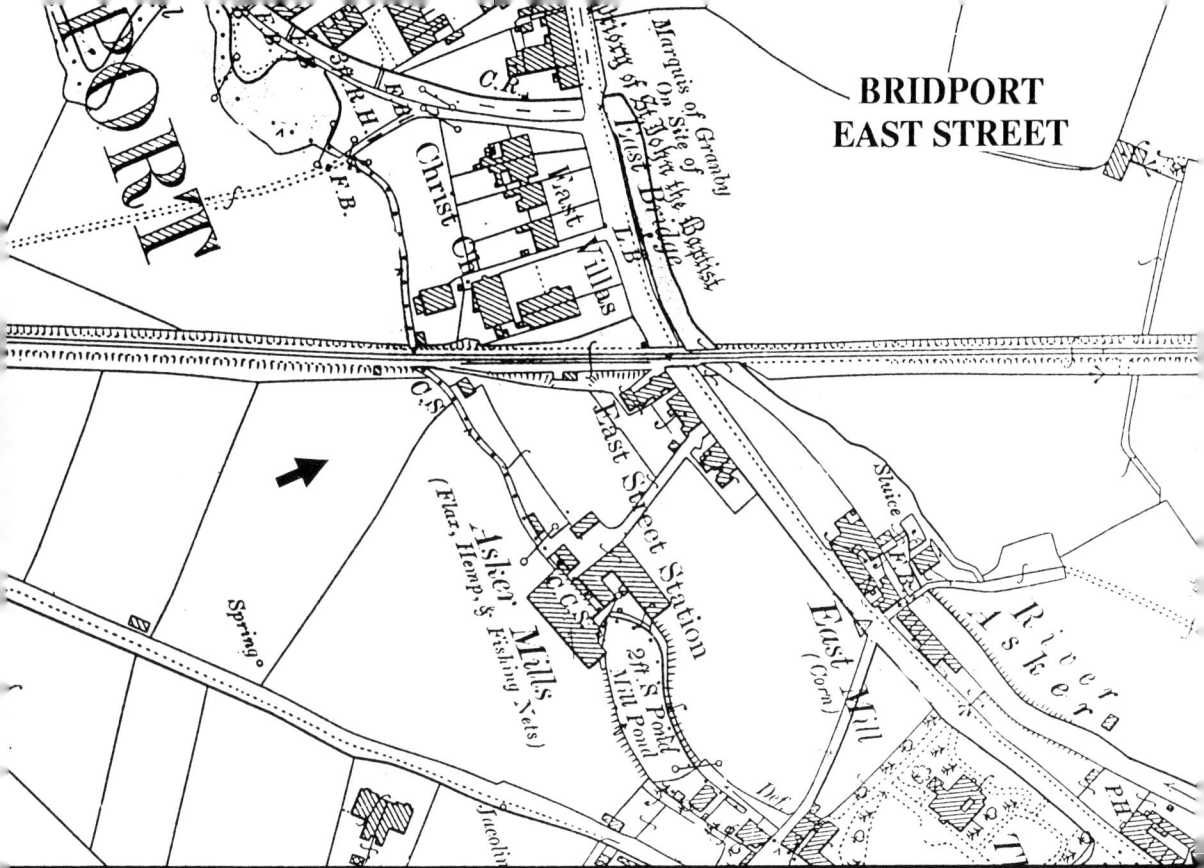

The 1901 map reveals much about local
industrial history.

92. A thatched cottage stood on the land
purchased for the railway construction and so
it was adapted for use as a booking office,
waiting room and station master's dwelling.
The hut housed a ground frame controlling the
crossing gates. (D.Cullum coll.)

93. Passenger services were provided between 31st March 1884 and 22nd September 1930, apart from a period during WWI. The thatched cottage was replaced in 1905 by the house seen in this southward view from the bridge over the River Asker. (Lens of Sutton)

95. A 1956 picture shows that the building was fenced off and used as a dwelling. The canopy of the main station can be seen in the distance. The track was lifted in March 1965. (S.C.Nash)

94. The station which remained intact long after the last passenger had departed, was more convenient to the town centre than the main one in Bradpole Road. The trackbed now forms part of the Bridport relief road. (Lens of Sutton)

WEST BAY

The 1901 survey marks the full extent of the village before it was developed as a small holiday resort. It did not grow into the "Bournemouth" that the promoters of the line from Bridport envisaged.

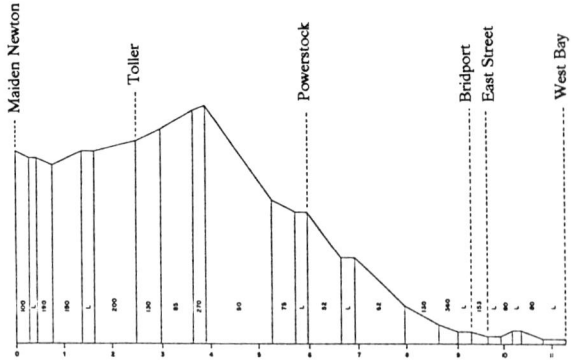

Maiden Newton — Toller — Powerstock — Bridport — East Street — West Bay

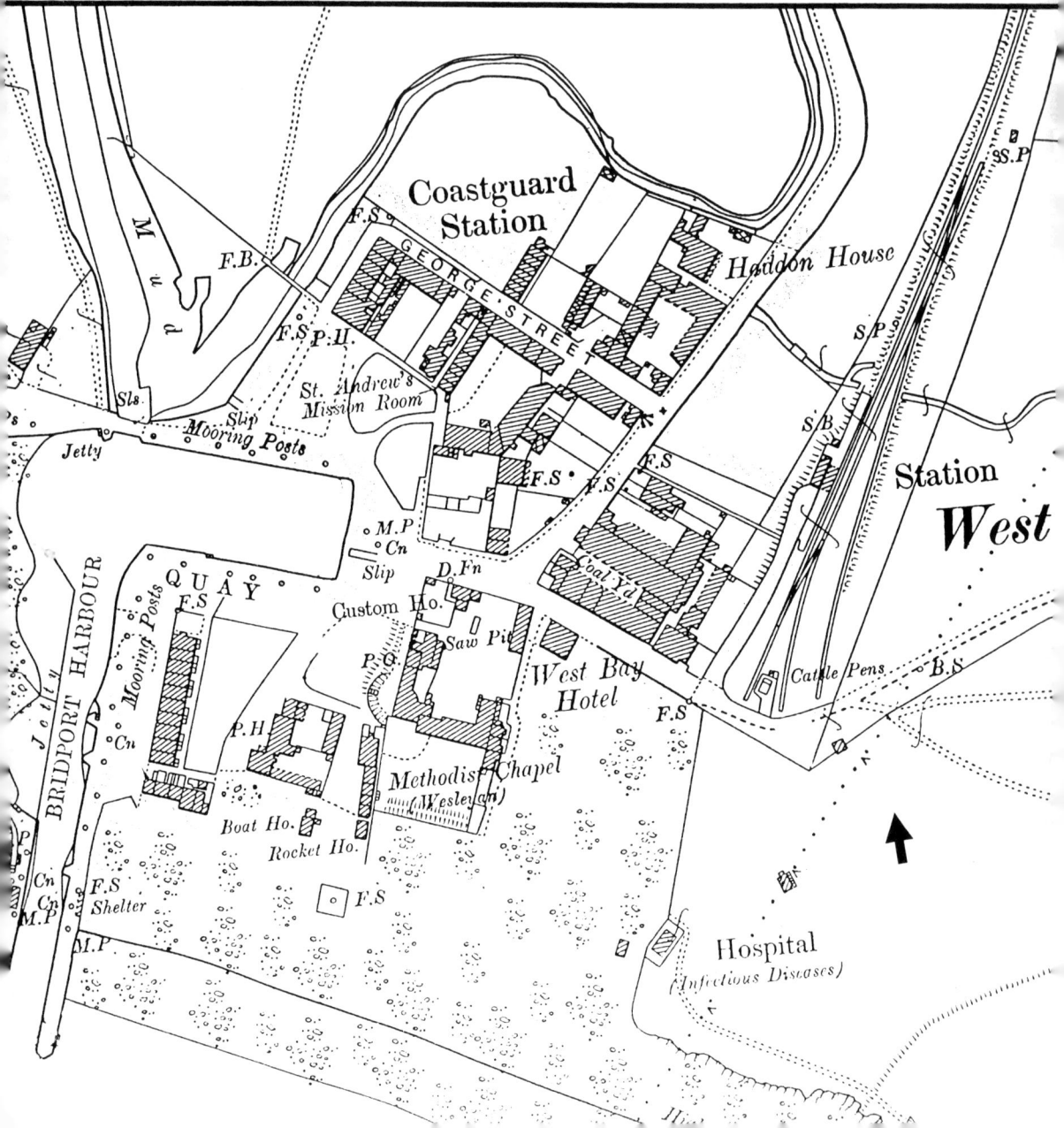

Coastguard Station

GEORGE STREET

Haddon House

F.B.

F.S.P.H.

St. Andrew's Mission Room

Mud

Sls

Jetty

Slip

Mooring Posts

S.P.

S.P.

S.B.

Station

West

F.S.

F.S.

F.S.

M.P

Cn

Slip

QUAY

Mooring Posts

F.S.

Cn

D.Fn

Custom Ho.

Coal Yd.

P.O.

Saw Pit

P.H.

West Bay Hotel

Cattle Pens

B.S.

F.S.

Methodist Chapel (Wesleyan)

BRIDPORT HARBOUR

Jetty

Boat Ho.

Rocket Ho.

Cn
Cb
M.P

F.S
Shelter

F.S

M.P.

Hospital
(Infectious Diseases)

West Bay, Bridport. No. 32

96. A panorama from East Cliff shows parts of the River Brit as it meanders down to Bridport Harbour. The dates for passenger traffic are the same as those given for East Street. Note the separate entrances for goods, cattle and passengers. (Lens of Sutton)

97. Freight services continued until 3rd December 1962, although latterly on a very limited scale. During WWII, the building was occupied by an engine driver and subsequently it was used by a firm of photographers. (Lens of Sutton)

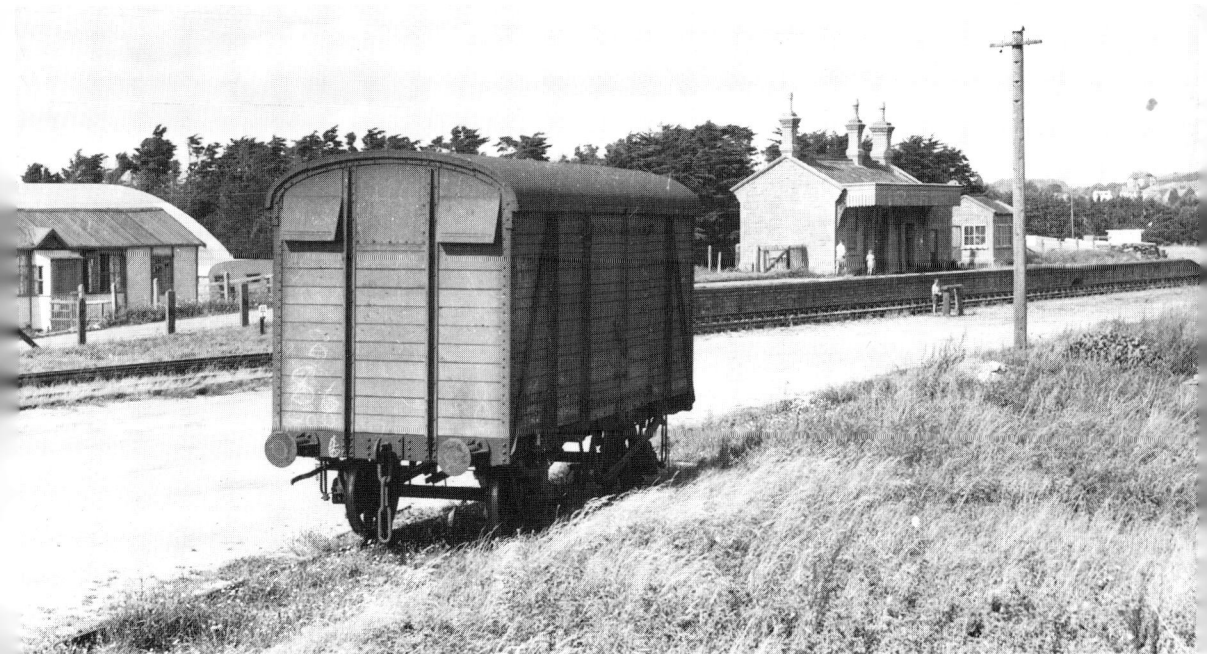

← 98. A 1956 picture shows that the permanent way was well cared for, no doubt at an expense much greater than the income from an occasional wagon load of gravel from the beach. The station was just over eleven miles from Maiden Newton. (S.C.Nash)

← 99. The Railway Enthusiasts Club railtour on 7th June 1958 was a very rare example of passengers being carried south of Bridport after 1932. The device to the left of the M7 is an elevator, used for loading shingle. (R.M.Casserley)

100. In May 1988, the buildings could be seen from the new car park. Even the stone-built signal box (left) survived. This had been down graded to a ground frame in January 1927 and the last station master left in November 1928. (V.Mitchell)

July 1925

LONDON, MAIDEN NEWTON, and BRIDPORT.—Great Western.

	Down.	Week Days.	Su		Up.	Week Days.	Su
		mrn|mrn| aft	mrn	aft	aft	aft |3 cl.	aft				mrn|mrn|mrn|	aft	aft	aft	aft		aft
2	London(Paddington)dep.	12 55	5 30	....	10 30	12 30	1 30	3 30	6 0	....	....	2 35	1½	Bridport (West Bay) ...dep.	....	10 20	....	....	12 15	2 35	....	6 0	....	....	c
—	Maiden Newton ....dep.	9 40	11 15	12 20	1 50	4 15	4 50	5	6 9	45	....	....	2 35	1	„ (East Street)......	....	10 25	....	....	12 20	2 40	....	6 5	....	....	
2½	Toller	9 46	11 21	12 26	1 56	4 21	4 56	8	6 9	53	....	....	2 42	2	„ for Lyme Regis {arr.	....	10 27	....	....	12 22	2 42	....	6 7	....	....	m
5½	Powerstock ....| 9 51|11 29|12 31| 2 4| 4 29| 5	4 8	14 10|3 |....|....|2 51			dep.| 8 50|10 30|11 40|....|12 22|2 55|3 50|....|7 10|....|....| 3 15
9½	B'port for Lyme Regis {arr.	10 1	11 36	12 41	2 11	4 36	5 11	8 2	10 12	....	....	2 58	5½	Powerstock	8 59	10 39	11 49	....	1 1	3 4	3 59	....	7 19	....	....	3 24
		dep.	10 8	11 42	....	2 16	....	5 20	....	....	....	....	d	8½	Toller	9 10	10 48	11 58	....	1 10	3 13	4 8	....	7 28	....	....	3 33
9½	„ (East Street)........	10 11	11 45	....	2 19	....	5 23	....	....	....	....		11½	Maiden Newton 2, 7....arr.	9 15	10 53	12 3	....	1 15	3 18	4 13	....	7 33	....	....	3 38
11½	„ (West Bay) ....arr.	10 14	11 49	....	2 23	....	5 27	....	....	....	....		15½	7 London(Paddington)arr.	12 55	3 25	3 35	....	....	6 50	8 10	....	2 40	....	....	7 45

A By Slip Carriage at Westbury.   c Runs to Weymouth (Town), see page 6.   d Starts from Weymouth (Town), see page 11.
H Except Mondays.   m Motor Car, one class only.

GRIMSTONE & FRAMPTON

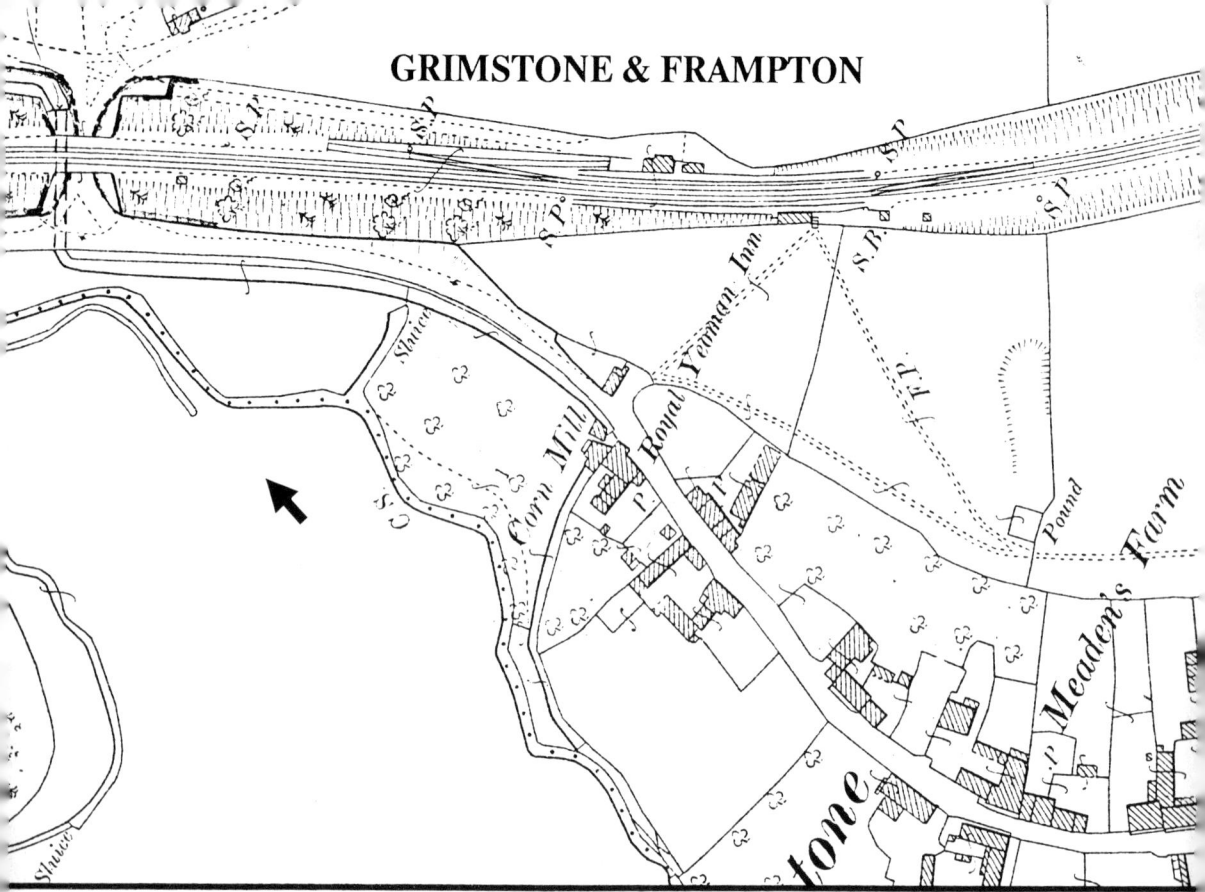

The 1902 edition indicates that footpaths gave access to the up side, whereas villagers had to take a circuitous route by road to the main buildings. The siding shown was replaced by one south of the down platform, in 1905.

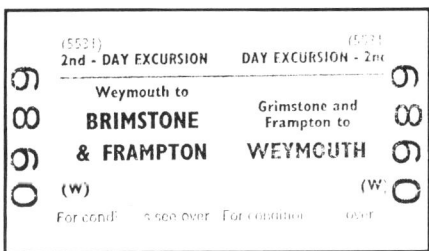

2nd - DAY EXCURSION   DAY EXCURSION - 2nd

Weymouth to

BRIMSTONE   Grimstone and
                  Frampton to
& FRAMPTON   **WEYMOUTH**

(W)   (W)

For cond⁰   see over   For condition   over

A rare spelling error on an issued ticket !

102. Bold quoins gave character to the brick-work and a series of five ornate lamps added charm to the up platform, as the line runs through reverse curves. (Lens of Sutton)

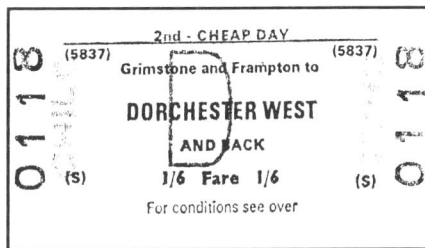

2nd - CHEAP DAY

(5837)   (5837)
Grimstone and Frampton to

DORCHESTER WEST

AND BACK

(S)   1/6 Fare 1/6   (S)

For conditions see over

101. The station opened with the line, although named Frampton initially, and was situated on the side of the Frome Valley. A down train is signalled, in this study of a lone passenger. (Lens of Sutton)

103. Another down train is signalled, as we examine the small coal yard on 27th September 1959. Half a mile to the right, the line passes through Frampton Tunnel. (C.L.Caddy)

104. No.6900 *Abney Hall* pounds up the gradient on 18th April 1964, bound for Bristol. The goods yard had been situated on the left and was closed on 1st May 1961. The 6 and 9 refer to the stopping position of diesel trains. (C.L.Caddy)

105. A southward view in May 1965 shows the well tended station before staffing ceased on 11th April 1966. Closure took place on 3rd October of that year and the buildings were demolished in 1967. (C.L.Caddy)

BRADFORD PEVERELL & STRATTON

106. The halt was close to the main road (A37) and half a mile from each village. It was opened on 22nd May 1933 and closed on 3rd October 1966. This is the southward view in 1963. (C.L.Caddy)

107. Like other halts on the route, it was first built with timber and replaced by concrete in 1959. Unlike the others, it remained intact in 1990, though somewhat overgrown. Here we look north, in July 1966. There has been a campaign recently to have the halt reopened, as there is much new housing in the area. (C.G.Maggs)

108. South of the halt, the line passes over the River Frome as it winds its way to its mouth at Wareham. A down freight rumbles over the 66yd viaduct on 26th March 1966. Before reaching Dorchester, the route passes under a Roman camp site, by means of the 264yd long Poundbury Tunnel. (J.Scrace)

Gt Western Ry   Gt Western Ry
Dorchester   Dorchester
TO
Bradford Peverell & Stratton
HALT
THIRD CLASS
6d C Fare 6d
Bradf'dPeverell&Strat'n Bradf'dPeverell&Strat'n
FOR CONDITIONS SEE BACK W.D
4856

2nd-SINGLE SINGLE-2nd

Dorchester West To
Dorchester W.   Dorchester W.
Bradford P. & S. H'lt   Bradford P.& S. H'lt
BRADFORD PEVERELL
& STRATTON HALT
(S)   6d.   FARE   6d.   (S)
For conditions see over For conditions see over
0894

DORCHESTER WEST

109. In the distance is the station's overall roof, which was removed in 1934. The siding in the foreground is laid on longtitudinal timbers, once a broad gauge practice, whereas the one on the left is conventionally timbered. The fresh chalk of the cutting suggests that this line was a late addition. (Lens of Sutton)

110. With Dorchester Barracks in the background, 2-6-0 no.6358 hauls its Bristol-Weymouth train past the signal box in 1956. "West" had been added to the station nameboard in November 1959. (J.W.T.House/C.L.Caddy)

111. Edisons operated a fleet of steam road rollers and ploughing engines and had their own siding on the SR (see below picture no.89 in our *Bournemouth to Weymouth* album).

One of their Avelings, with chimney removed, provides entertainment for some of the local youth as it creeps onto a Lowmac, on its way to a scrapyard. (R.B.Gosling/C.L.Caddy)

112. No.5996 *Mytton Hall* departs for Bristol on 10th July 1956 and passes over the crossover adjacent to the down refuge siding. Diesel-

isation was then only three years away. (R.C.Riley)

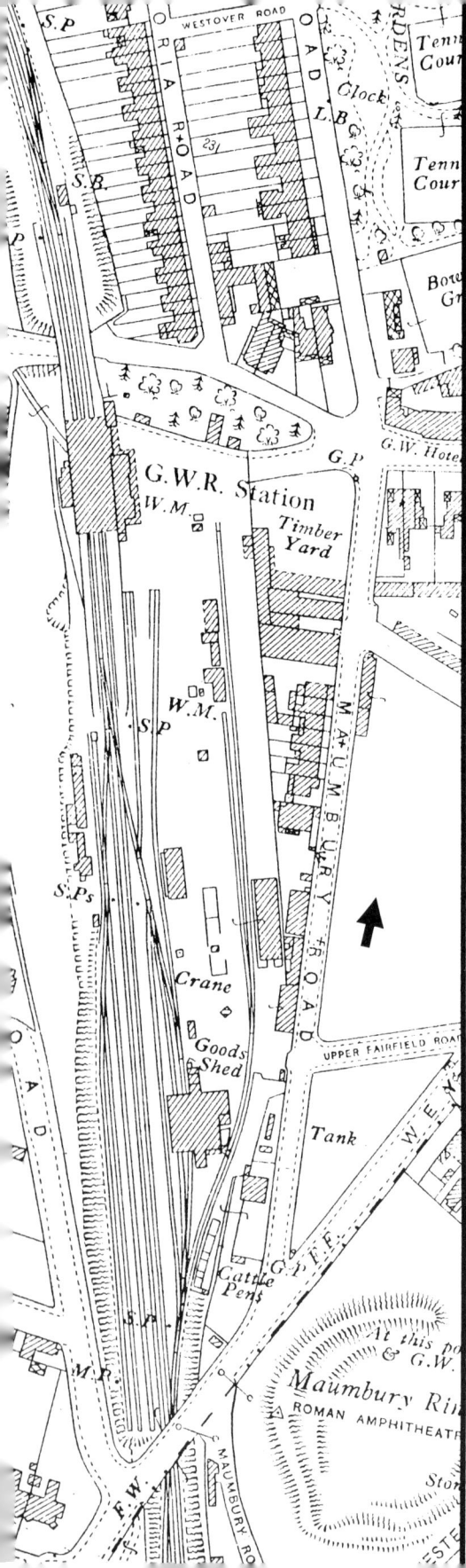

The 1929 map shows the layout at its optimum with the 250yd long down refuge siding diverging near the top edge and the 320yd long Cemetery Siding at the bottom. This was in reality a loop and was used for the transfer of wagons between the SR and GWR. The crane shown was of 6 ton capacity.

113. The panorama from the Weymouth Road bridge on the same day includes the castle-like baracks and class 4300 2-6-0 no.5323 passing a SR rail-built signal. The GWR's no.4090 *Dorchester Castle* was named after a structure that did not exist! (R.C.Riley)

114. A 1963 northward view shows the SR style nameboard, the Southern Region having been responsible for the station since 1950. Note the kink in the up platform coping, necessary to give clearance for locomotives using the crossover. (C.L.Caddy)

115. The entrance was still gaslit when photographed in 1968. Architect Ritson's design features included a hipped roof, deep eaves and round headed windows. The station lost its staff on 2nd January 1972. (C.L.Caddy)

116. The signal box is seen in 1971 but it had been closed on 9th June 1968. The line south of Maiden Newton is worked by tokenless block, the nearest signalman being at Dorchester South. (J.Scrace)

117. The 17.43 Weymouth to Bristol on 7th July 1971 passes the site of the goods yard, which was closed to traffic on 6th September 1965 and was disconnected in 1968. Cattle traffic had been transferred to the South station in 1950. (J.Scrace)

118. No.D1009 *Western Invader* waits to depart for Weymouth on 23rd April 1975. Double track has been retained south from Dorchester West almost to the junction. (J.Scrace)

119. Bound for Bristol on 6th December 1986, unit no.B430 passes onto the single line, near the site of the former signal box. The unit was painted chocolate and cream, as part of the commemoration of the 150th anniversary of the founding of the GWR. (M.Turvey)

120. The 15.06 from Bristol Temple Meads on 2nd August 1989 stands at the down platform, the building of which was shedding the rendering from its stonework. It had been sold by BR but, being a listed structure, it could not be demolished. In January 1990, renovation work commenced. Although used by Provincial trains, the station is the responsibility of Network SouthEast who gave passengers accommodation once again, thus encouraging them to use the improved services. (J.H.Bird)

MP *Middleton Press*

Easebourne Lane, Midhurst. West Sussex. GU29 9AZ
(0730) 813169

BRANCH LINES

BRANCH LINES TO MIDHURST
BRANCH LINES AROUND MIDHURST
BRANCH LINES TO HORSHAM
BRANCH LINES TO EAST GRINSTEAD
BRANCH LINES TO ALTON
BRANCH LINE TO HAYLING
BRANCH LINE TO SOUTHWOLD
BRANCH LINE TO TENTERDEN
BRANCH LINES TO NEWPORT
BRANCH LINES TO TUNBRIDGE WELLS
BRANCH LINE TO SWANAGE
BRANCH LINES TO LONGMOOR
BRANCH LINE TO LYME REGIS
BRANCH LINE TO FAIRFORD
BRANCH LINE TO ALLHALLOWS
BRANCH LINES AROUND ASCOT
BRANCH LINES AROUND WEYMOUTH
BRANCH LINE TO HAWKHURST
BRANCH LINES AROUND EFFINGHAM JNC

SOUTH COAST RAILWAYS

CHICHESTER TO PORTSMOUTH
BRIGHTON TO EASTBOURNE
RYDE TO VENTNOR
EASTBOURNE TO HASTINGS
PORTSMOUTH TO SOUTHAMPTON
HASTINGS TO ASHFORD
SOUTHAMPTON TO BOURNEMOUTH
ASHFORD TO DOVER
BOURNEMOUTH TO WEYMOUTH
DOVER TO RAMSGATE

SOUTHERN MAIN LINES

HAYWARDS HEATH TO SEAFORD
EPSOM TO HORSHAM
CRAWLEY TO LITTLEHAMPTON
THREE BRIDGES TO BRIGHTON
WATERLOO TO WOKING
VICTORIA TO EAST CROYDON
TONBRIDGE TO HASTINGS
EAST CROYDON TO THREE BRIDGES
WOKING TO SOUTHAMLPTON
WATERLOO TO WINDSOR
LONDON BRIDGE TO EAST CROYDON

COUNTRY RAILWAY ROUTES

BOURNEMOUTH TO EVERCREECH JNC
READING TO GUILDFORD
WOKING TO ALTON
BATH TO EVERCREECH JUNCTION
GUILDFORD TO REDHILL
EAST KENT LIGHT RAILWAY
FAREHAM TO SALISBURY
BURNHAM TO EVERCREECH JUNCTION
REDHILL TO ASHFORD
YEOVIL TO DORCHESTER

LONDON SUBURBAN RAILWAYS

CHARING CROSS TO DARTFORD

STEAMING THROUGH

STEAMING THROUGH EAST HANTS
STEAMING THROUGH SURREY
STEAMING THROUGH WEST SUSSEX
STEAMING THROUGH THE ISLE OF WIGHT
STEAMING THROUGH WEST HANTS

OTHER RAILWAY BOOKS

GARRAWAY FATHER & SON
LONDON CHATHAM & DOVER RAILWAY
INDUSTRIAL RAILWAYS OF THE S. EAST
WEST SUSSEX RAILWAYS IN THE 1980S

OTHER BOOKS

MIDHURST TOWN THEN & NOW
EAST GRINSTEAD THEN & NOW

WALKS IN THE WESTERN HIGH WEALD

MILITARY DEFENCE OF WEST SUSSEX
TILLINGBOURNE BUS STORY

SURREY WATERWAYS
KENT AND EAST SUSSEX WATERWAYS